Lincolnshire

COUNTY COUNCIL

discover libraries

**This book should be returned on or before
the due date.**

30. MAR 16.

NCI 10/17

NE 4/18

STAMFORD LIBRARY

9/18 Tel: 01522 782010

GRANTHAM LIBRARY

- 6 FEB 2019

01522 782010

To renew or order library books please telephone 01522 782010
or vi~~~~~ ~~~~~~~~~~~~~~~~~~~~~

You will r~~~~~ ~~~~~~~~~~~~~~~~ ~ber.

The above doe~~~~~ ~~~~~~~~ion Stock.

D1422699

MRS BEETON'S GUIDE

TO

EMBROIDERY CROCHET *and* KNITTING

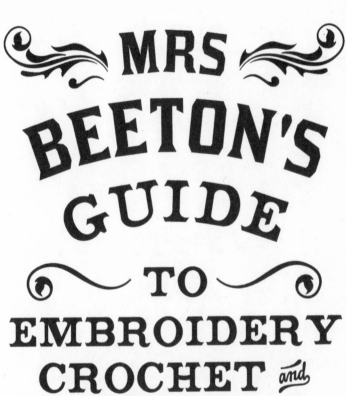

MRS BEETON'S GUIDE

TO

EMBROIDERY CROCHET *and* KNITTING

AMBERLEY

First published 1870
This edition first published 2015

Amberley Publishing
The Hill, Stroud
Gloucestershire, GL5 4EP

www.amberley-books.com

Copyright © Amberley Publishing 2015

The right of Amberley Publishing to be identified as the Author
of this work has been asserted in accordance with the
Copyrights, Designs and Patents Act 1988.

British Library Cataloguing in Publication Data.
A catalogue record for this book is available from the British Library.

ISBN 978 1 4456 4422 6 (hardback)
ISBN 978 1 4456 4435 6 (ebook)

Typeset in 10pt on 12pt Sabon.
Typesetting and Origination by Fakenham Prepress Solutions.
Printed in the UK.

Embroidery

Embroidery Instructions

The art of embroidering with cotton on linen, muslin, cambric, piqué, &c., is very easy to learn by strictly attending to the following instructions.

The size of the thread and needle must correspond to that of the material on which you embroider; the needle must not be too long, and the cotton must be soft. Messrs. Walter Evans and Co.'s embroidery cotton is the best. Skilful embroiderers never work over anything, because when you tack the material on paper or cloth each stitch shows, and if the material is very fine, leaves small holes; but for those that are learning we should advise them to tack the material to be embroidered upon a piece of *toile cirée*. If you work without this, place the material straight over the forefinger of the left hand; the material must never he held slantways. The three other fingers of the left hand hold the work; the thumb remains free to give the right position to each stitch. The work must always, if possible, lie so that the outline of the pattern is turned towards the person who works. For the sake of greater clearness one part of the following illustrations is given in larger size than nature. Preparing the patterns is one of the most important things in embroidery, for the shape of the patterns is often spoiled merely because they have not been prepared with sufficient care.

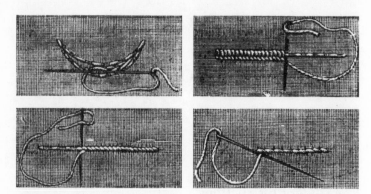

Top left: 1. Scallop: This illustration shows how to prepare a scallop. Take thicker cotton than that with which you work; never commence with a knot, and do not take a thread longer than sixteen or eighteen inches. The outlines of the scallops are first traced with short straight stitches. In the corners particularly the stitches must be short. The space between the outlines is filled with chain stitches, as can be seen from the illustration; they must not be too long, otherwise the embroidery will look coarse. It is in this way that every pattern to be worked in button-hole or satin stitch is to be prepared.

Top right: 2. Double Overcast Stitch: This illustration shows the double overcast stitch or button-hole stitch in a straight line. After having traced the outline begin to work from left to right; fasten the cotton with a few stitches, hold it with the thumb of the left hand under the outline, insert the needle downwards above the outline, draw it out under the same above the cotton which you hold in the left hand, and draw it up. Repeat for all the stitches in the same manner; they must be regular and lie close to one another. Great care should be taken that the material on which you embroider is not puckered.

Bottom left: 3. Overcast Stitch: The double overcast and the button-hole stitches are worked from left to right, whilst back stitches, knotted and satin stitches are worked from right to left. The stitch is worked in the same way as the double overcast, only the needle must never be drawn out in overcast stitching, but in slanting overcast stitching, the cotton with which you work, and which you keep down with the thumb of the left hand.

Bottom right: 4. Slanting Overcast Stitch: The slanting overcast stitch is worked without tracing the outline, always inserting the needle downwards – that is, from top to bottom. The needle must be inserted in the manner shown in the illustration – that is, not straight, but slanting; insert it a little farther than the last stitch, and draw it out close to it. The wrong side of the work must show back stitches. This sort of stitch is used for the fine outlines in patterns or letters.

Embroidery

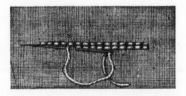

5. Back Stitch: This shows the back stitch, the working of which is well known; it is worked in several rows close to each other.

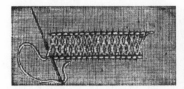
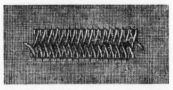

6 and 7. *Point Croisé*: These two illustrations show another kind of back stitch, called *point croisé*, which is only used on very thin and transparent materials. This stitch forms on the wrong side a sort of darned pattern, which is seen by transparence on the right side, and gives the embroidered pattern a thicker appearance, contrasting with the rest of the work (see the lower leaves of the flower on illustration 45). For this stitch insert the needle into the material as for the common back stitch, draw it out underneath the needle on the opposite outline of the patter, so as to form on the wrong side a slanting line. Insert the needle again as for common back stitch; draw it out slanting at the place marked for the next stitch on the opposite outline, as shown in illustration 6.

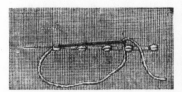
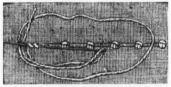

Left: 8. Knotted Stitch: This illustration shows the knotted stitch; the simplest way of working it is to work two back stitches at a short distance from each other over the same thread.

Right: 9. Knotted Stitch: The knotted stitch seen in this illustration is worked thus: take about four threads of the material on the needle, draw the needle half out, wind the cotton twice round the point of the needle, hold it tight with the thumb, draw the needle out carefully and insert it at the place where the stitch was begun, and draw it out at the place where the next stitch is to be worked.

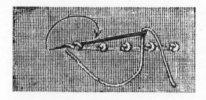

10. Knotted Stitch: The knotted stitch seen in this illustration is worked in nearly the same manner as the preceding one. Before drawing the cotton out of the material hold it tight with the left-hand thumb; leave the needle in the same position, wind the cotton twice round it, turn the needle from left to right, so (follow the direction of the arrow) that its point arrives where the cotton was drawn out (marked by a cross in illustration), insert the needle there, and draw it out at the place of the next stitch.

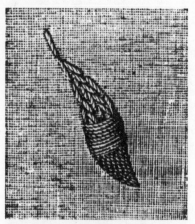

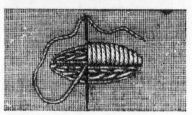

11 and 12. Raised Satin Stitch: Raised satin stitch is principally used for blossoms, flowers, leaves, letters, &c. After having traced the outlines of the pattern, fill the space left between them with chain stitches in a direction different from that in which the pattern is to be embroidered; begin at the point of the leaf, working from right to left, make short straight stitches, always inserting the needle close above the outline and drawing it out below. The leaves on the flowers, as well as on the branches, must be begun from the point, because they thus acquire a better shape. If you wish to work a leaf divided in the middle, as seen in illustration 12, you must trace the veining before you fill it with chain stitches, then begin at one point of the leaf and work first one half and then the other.

13. *Point de plume*: This illustration shows the so-called *point de plume* on a scalloped leaf. It is worked like the satin stitch, only the needle is drawn through the material in a slanting direction.

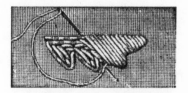

14. *Point de Minute*: This stitch is often used instead of satin stitch when the patterns must appear raised. Wind the cotton several times round the point of the needle, which is inserted into the material half its length (the number of times the cotton is to be wound round the needle depends on the length of the pattern), hold fast the windings with the thumb of the left hand, draw the needle and the cotton through the windings, insert the needle into the material at the same place, and draw it out at the place where the next stitch is to begin.

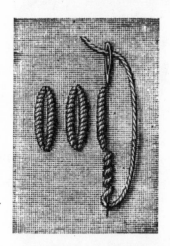

15 and 16. Ladder Stitch: These two illustration show the *ladder stitch*, often used in ornamental embroidery. Trace first the outlines as seen in illustration; mark also the cross stitches between the outlines, so that the first touch the outlines only at both ends. The outlines are embroidered in overcast stitch or double overcast; the material is cut away underneath the ladder stitch between the outlines.

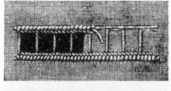

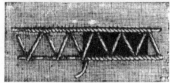

We have now shown the different kinds of stitches used in embroidery; the following instructions show them used for different patterns.

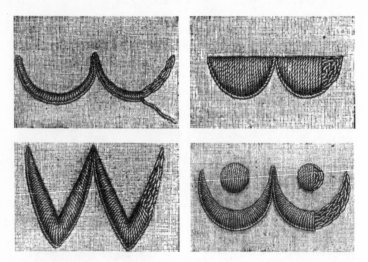

17–20. Button-Hole Stitch Scallop: These scallops are prepared as above described. Take care to have the stitches even and regular; the scallops must be wide in the centre and very fine at both ends.

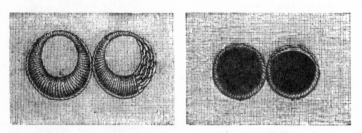

21 and 22. Button and Eyelet Holes: This kind of embroidery is used only in round or long patterns. Trace first the outline of the hole, cut away a small round piece of material, not too close to the outlines (when the button-hole is very small merely insert the point of the scissors or a stiletto into the material), fold the edge of the material back with the needle, and work the hole in overcast stitch, inserting the needle into the empty place in the centre and drawing it out under the outline. Some button-holes are worked separately; sometimes they are in a row; if so, take care to begin to work each button-hole at the place where it touches the next. In the following button-holes the outside must be traced double, so as to reach as far as the next one, but each button-hole is finished at once. Illustration 21 shows a button-hole worked round in a button-hole stitch, 22 an eyelet-hole worked in overcast.

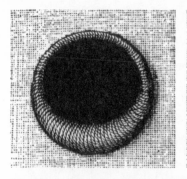
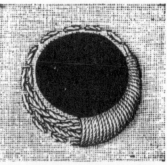

23 and 24. Shaded Button-Hole: Shaded button-holes are worked like the others, only they are prepared, as can be seen in illustration 24, so as to mark the thickness. The stitches must gradually get narrower or wider, and be worked very close to each other.

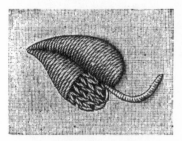
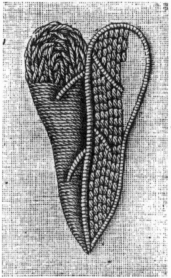

25 and 26. Leaf in Raised Satin Stitch: In a leaf like the one seen in illustration 26 work first the outline and veining in overcast stitch; work one half of the leaf in satin stitch, and the other half between the overcast outline and veining in back stitch. The stem of a leaf is always worked last.

27 and 28. Raised Leaf: For leaves like the one seen in illustration 28 begin with the veinings, then work the inner points, then the outer ones, and lastly the raised spots in the centre. The leaf seen in illustration 27 is worked, one half in *point de plume*, the other half in back stitch or *point d'or*.

29. Leaf: The outline of this leaf is embroidered in overcast stitch; the open-work veining consists of eyelets; one half of the leaf is worked in back stitch, the other half in a kind of satin stitch worked without chain stitches underneath; the stitches are worked across the leaf, leaving between two stitches an interval as wide as the stitch itself. The next row is then worked in these intervals, and each stitch begins half-way up the one before and after it.

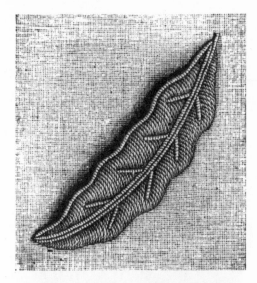

30–32. Leaf

Raised: This kind of embroidery is particularly beautiful, as it is worked separately and sewn on the material with an outline in very fine cotton; this produces the shade seen in 30 (see also illustration 33 and 48). For such leaves work first one half in overcast and satin stitch (illustration 31); the other half is worked on a separate piece of material (see illustration 32); cut away the material along the overcast outline, and fasten it on the foundation material along the outline which forms the veining on illustration 31.

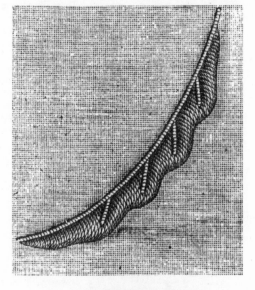

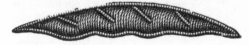

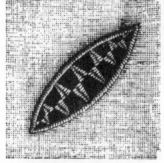

33–35. Raised Embroidered Leaf:
These illustrations show a similar leaf;
both halves are worked separately
(see illustration 34); the centre is
worked in open lace stitch. The latter
(see illustration 35) is traced, then
make ladder stitches across, work
the outlines in overcast stitch, and
cut away the material underneath the
ladder stitch. The cross stitches are
then worked in darning stitch with
very fine cotton wherever two threads
meet.

36. Blossom in Satin Stitch: The eyelet
is worked in overcast stitch, then work
the upper part of the blossom all in
one piece as far as the beginning of the
veining, thence the blossom is worked
in two halves.

37 and 38. Blossom in Satin Stitch: The raised centre of this flower is formed by a bead, over which the embroidery is worked. When the leaves have been worked one after the other, place a bead in the centre, left free in such a manner that one hole lies on the material, and work over the bead by inserting the needle into its upper hole, then underneath the material, drawing it out above the material close to the bead, and so on (see illustration 38).

39. Star in Satin Stitch: The centre, which forms a wheel, is worked first. Draw the threads across the circle marked by an outline; in the centre they are wound round, always taking one thread *on the needle* and leaving the next thread *under the needle*, as can be seen in 57 on the half-finished pattern. The material underneath the wheel is only cut away when the rest of the pattern has been embroidered.

40 and 41. Stars: The small star in the centre of illustration 40 is worked in *point de reprise*.

42. Flower in Satin Stitch: The fine veinings are worked with fine black silk in *point Russe*, which renders the effect of the flower very beautiful.

 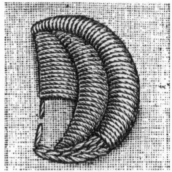

43 and 44. Rose in Satin Stitch: Illustration 44 shows one petal larger than full size. The outer circle only is prepared with chain stitches underneath, so as to appear raised; the inner circles are worked flat. The centre of the rose is embroidered in open work.

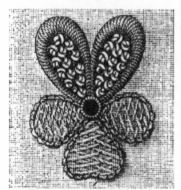 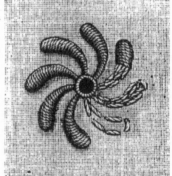

Left: 45. Embroidered Heartsease: For the knotted stitch see illustration 10, for the *point croisé* see 6 and 7.

Right: 46. Flower in Raised Satin Stitch

47. An Ear of Corn in *Point de Minute*

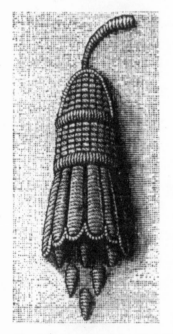

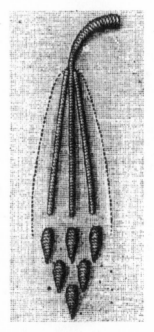

48 and 49. Bluebell in Raised Satin Stitch: This flower is worked partly in separate pieces, as has been described. Illustration 51 shows the raised part stretched out flat. When it is finished it is fastened down along the dotted line on illustration 49, which shows the inner part of the flower.

50. Flower in *Point de Minute*:
This stitch is here worked over a
thick foundation of chain stitches.
For raised patterns it looks very
well.

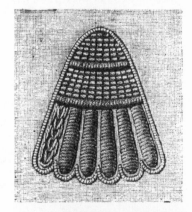

51 and 52. Flower Worked in
Appliqué: To work in appliqué,
two materials, either similar or
different, are needed. You can
work either in appliqué of muslin
on muslin, or of muslin on net, or
of net on net. Muslin on Brussels
net is the prettiest way of working
in appliqué; we will therefore
describe it: the other materials
are worked in the same manner.
Trace the pattern on the muslin,
fasten the latter on the net, and
trace the outlines of the pattern
with very small stitches. Work
them in overcast stitch with very
fine cotton, taking care not to
pucker the material. The veinings
are worked in overcast. When the
pattern has been embroidered cut
away the muslin round the outlines
with sharp scissors, so that the
net forms the grounding (see No.
52). The greatest care is required
in cutting out the muslin to avoid
touching the threads of the net.

 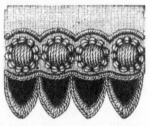

53 and 54. Narrow Borders: It will be easy to work these borders from the above instructions. Observe only that on border 53 the outer row of scallops is worked first, then the button-hole stitch row, and the rest afterwards. The spots are edged all round in knotted stitch. The wheels in the centre of the eyelets of No. 54 are worked with very fine cotton in loose button-hole stitch; they are wound round with the cotton in a second row.

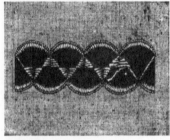

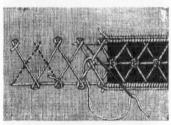

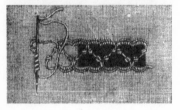

55–57. Insertion: Three strips of insertion, which are worked nearly like the ladder stitch. For No. 55, in tracing the outlines, make two small knots at short distances by winding the cotton four times round the needle, as can be seen in the illustration; the windings are held down with the thumb of the left hand, draw the needle through, and a knot is formed. The outlines are worked in button-hole stitch only when all the knots have been made, and then the material is cut away underneath. Illustration 56 is a variety of the slanting ladder stitch. In illustration 57 the cross threads are worked in two rows in the common herring-bone stitch, as can be seen by the black lines on the illustration. The straight lines at the top and at the bottom are worked in double overcast; lastly, the wheels are worked in a row as described for the star pattern, No. 39.

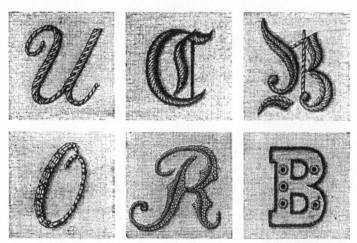

58–64. Embroidered Initials: To learn to work
initials the Roman characters are the easiest to
begin with. They must be traced and prepared
like other embroidery in satin stitch, only the
chain stitches underneath must not be too thick;
it would take away the shape of the letters. All
depends on the fineness and regularity of the
stitches; they must be worked in overcast stitch.
Work from left to right, and the letter when
completed must look rather like raised printing
than like embroidery. Gothic letters are much
more difficult to work on account of the many

flourishes; it requires great practice in needlework to embroider them well.
The small black dots in illustration 58 are worked in black silk on the thick
parts of the letter: the fine strokes are covered with cross threads of black
silk. The outlines of the letter in illustration 59 and the fine strokes are
worked in black silk. The letter in illustration 60 is embroidered in raised
satin stitch and *point de plume*. The letter in illustration 61 is worked in
back stitches, over which are worked at regular distances cross stitches of
black silk. Illustration 62 shows a letter in satin and back stitch. Illustration
63 to be worked in overcast and double overcast. Illustration 64 is a letter
G in *Point Russe* with black silk.

65. Embroidered Figures: They are worked like the letters in *point de plume* and overcast; the dots are worked in knotted stitch.

In working the following Embroidery Patterns it will be found advisable to trace the design clearly upon tracing-paper with a sharp-pointed lead pencil. The pattern thus traced must be perforated with a fine needle in a succession of tiny holes, at the rate of about twenty to the inch. Those ladies who possess a sewing-machine will find no difficulty in accomplishing this. Several thicknesses of paper can be perforated at the same time, if required, by any ordinary machine. To transfer the traced and perforated design to the fabric to be embroidered, it is only necessary to rub a small quantity of powder blue through the holes.

Insertion in Embroidery

Material: Messrs. Walter Evans and Co.'s embroidery cotton No. 16.

This insertion is worked in raised satin stitch and button-hole stitch. The outlines must first be traced and the space filled up with chain stitches. To work a leaf, begin at

66. Insertion in Embroidery.

the point, working from right to left, making short stitches, and always inserting the needle close above the outline and drawing it out below. The holes left for the ribbon to pass through are worked in plain button-hole stitch, the dots are worked in raised satin stitch.

Insertion in Embroidery and Stitching

Materials: Messrs. Walter Evans and Co.'s embroidery cotton Nos. 10 and 16.

The veinings of this pretty insertion must be worked in overcast stitch (No. 3), the leaves and flowers in raised satin stitch, the scallops in button-hole stitch, and the outer edge of the leaves in back stitch (No. 5) with No. 10 cotton.

67. Insertion in Embroidery and Stitching.

Cravat End in Embroidery

Materials: Muslin, cambric, or linen; Messrs. Walter Evans and Co.'s embroidery cotton No. 24, or fine black China silk.

This graceful design is worked in raised satin stitch (see Nos. 11 and 12) and back stitching, or point Russe. Black silk may be introduced at will, and the delicate leaves may be stitched in fine black silk, and the flowers embroidered in white, with the stamens in black silk.

68. Embroidered Pattern for Cravat Ends, &c.

Basket Embroidered in Chenille

Materials: A basket of fine wicker-work; 1 skein of black chenille, and 3 of blue chenille.

This small round basket measures seven inches across; it has a cover and two handles. The wicker is very delicately plaited, and is ornamented with a pattern in chenille which is very easy to work. Upon the cover, work in point Russe one large star in blue chenille, with the centre and outer circle in black. All round, work small stars in blue chenille, with a black stitch in the centre. The position of these stars is shown in our illustration. The basket requires no mounting; it is not even lined.

69. Basket Embroidered in Chenille.

Pattern for Collars and Cuffs in Embroidery

Materials: Muslin, cambric or lawn; Messrs. Walter Evans and Co.'s embroidery cotton perfectionné No. 40.

Work the outer circle in long even scallops (see 17–20) in raised button-hole stitch; the spray of flowers is embroidered in raised satin stitch, the leaves in the same, and the rosebud calyx in tiny eyelet-holes. The centres of the roses are embroidered in open-work.

70. Embroidery Pattern for Collars, Cuffs, &c.

Cravat End in Embroidery

Materials: Muslin, Brussels net; Messrs. Walter Evans and Co.'s embroidery cotton No. 30.

Tack the traced muslin over the net and work the scallop of the inner edge; next the design in the centre must be worked in raised satin stitch (see 11 and 12). The raised dots are also worked in satin stitch. Lastly, work the outer edging of round scallops and the lines of raised dots, and with a pair of embroidery scissors carefully cut away the muslin from the outer edge and from the leaves of the centre pattern.

71. Cravat End in Embroidery.

Embroidery Pattern for Collars, Cuffs, &c.

72. Embroidery Pattern for Collars, Cuffs, &c.

Materials: Linen; Messrs. Walter Evans and Co.'s cotton perfectionné No. 40.

This pretty star should be worked in fine overcast stitch (see No. 3). The centre is worked in raised satin stitch leaves round a circle of button-hole stitch, in the middle of which a wheel is worked thus: Slip the cotton under the thick edge and fasten it, then cross it over and back so as to make 8 bars, then twist the cotton twice round 1 bar; this will bring it to the centre; work over and under each of the bars until a thick dot is formed; fasten the cotton beneath this, and twist it twice round the bar opposite to the first one you worked, and finish off.

Embroidery Covering for a Quilted Counterpane

Materials: Cashmere, cambric muslin, or linen; Messrs. Walter Evans and Co.'s embroidery cotton No. 4.

73. Embroidery Covering for a Quilted Counterpart.

This is an embroidery-pattern for a woollen or silk quilted counterpane. Such counterpanes generally have a lining which is turned back on the right side, and buttoned down at the point of each scallop. The pattern is a quilted counterpane of scarlet cashmere; the lining is of fine linen. Before embroidering it, make the points for the corners. The embroidery is worked in button-hole stitch, overcast, satin, and ladder stitch. It can also be worked on fine cambric or muslin, and then the embroidered pattern sewn on the piece of linen which forms the cover on the wrong side. Make the button-holes as seen in the illustration, and sew on mother-of-pearl or china buttons.

Embroidery Pattern for Ornamenting Collars, Cuffs, &c.

Materials: Muslin, cambric, or linen; Messrs. Walter Evans and Co.'s embroidery cotton No. 40.

This pattern is worked in satin stitch, point Russe, and point d'or on muslin, cambric, or linen; it is suitable for collars, or cravat ends, or handkerchief corners.

74. Embroidery Pattern for Cravat Ends, &c.

Handkerchief in Embroidery

Materials: French cambric; Messrs. Walter Evans and Co.'s embroidery cotton No. 50.

Three rows of hem-stitching ornament this handkerchief; the pattern forms an insertion within the outer rows, the flowers are worked in raised satin stitch, with eyelet-hole centres (see No. 22); the tendrils are worked in overcast stitch; three rows of raised dots, in groups of four, are worked on

75. Handkerchief in Embroidery.

the inner side of the last row of hem-stitching. This pattern looks very handsome on a broad-hemmed handkerchief.

Convolvulus Leaf Insertion

Materials: Muslin; Messrs. Walter Evans and Co.'s embroidery cotton No. 20.

The convolvulus leaves are worked in raised satin stitch, the veinings and stems in overcast stitch, the eyelet-holes in slanting overcast stitch. (See No. 4)

76. Convolvulus Leaf Insertion.

Insertion

Materials: Muslin; Messrs. Walter Evans and Co.'s embroidery cotton No. 20.

This simple insertion is worked in raised satin stitch, the stems alone excepted; these are embroidered in overcast stitch.

77. Insertion.

Two Patterns in Embroidery for Trimming Lingerie

Materials: Messrs. Walter Evans and Co.'s embroidery cotton No. 20, and Mecklenburg thread No. 50.

These patterns are worked in point Russe and stitching; the spots in satin and knotted stitch. Illustration 13 is ornamented in the centre with lace stitches.

78 and 79. Patterns for Trimming Lingerie.

Insertion

Materials: Muslin; Messrs. Walter Evans and Co.'s embroidery cotton No. 16.

The two insertions, Nos. 15 and 16, are worked partly in satin stitch, partly in open-work embroidery, and are edged on either side with an open-work hem.

80 and 81. Insertion.

Couvrette in Appliqué Embroidery

Materials: Net, fine muslin; Messrs. Walter Evans and Co.'s embroidery cotton No. 16.

The pattern must be traced on the muslin, which should be tacked on the net. The outline of the design must be traced with very small stitches, and worked in overcast stitches, as are also the veinings; the dots are worked in raised satin stitch; the border is embroidered with satin stitch flowers and scallop button-hole stitch. To work appliqué on net, see No. 52 of 'Embroidery Instructions'.

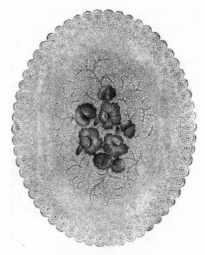

82. Couvrette in Appliqué Embroidery.

Wreath for Centre of Pincushion or Toilet Mat

Materials for Pincushion: Jaconet muslin; Messrs. Walter Evans and Co.'s embroidery cotton No. 16. For toilet mat: White piqué; cotton No. 12.

83. Wreath for Centre of Pincushion or Toilet Mat.

The leaves and flowers are worked in satin stitch; the eyelet-holes and stems in overcast stitch.

Corner for Handkerchief in Point Russe

Materials: French cambric, fine China black sewing-silk, or filoselle.

Point Russe stitch is made by a succession of back stitches. These stitches carefully follow every line of the design, and are worked in black China sewing-silk or filoselle. The pattern should be repeated at each corner of the handkerchief.

84. Corner for Handkerchief in Point Russe.

Borders and Insertions – White Embroidery

Materials: Lawn; Messrs. Walter Evans and Co.'s embroidery cotton No. 30, and Mecklenburg thread No. 50; fine black sewing-silk.

For the border No. 85, trace first the outlines of the scallop, then draw the threads which are to form the wheel in each scallop (take for this fine Mecklenburg thread, for the rest embroidery cotton), fasten them at the places where they cross each other, and work at these places small and large spots in satin stitch. Then work the scallops in button-hole stitch; edge each larger spot with button-hole stitch all round, and make a row of button-hole stitches for the upper edge of the border, and above this a row of herring-bone stitches. The material is cut away underneath the wheels.

85. Embroidered Border.

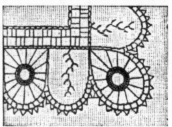

86 and 87. Corner in Embroidery.

The corner borders, illustrations 86 and 87, are worked in point Russe, chain and satin stitch, with fine black sewing silk.

Muslin Cravat

Materials: Muslin; Messrs. Walter Evans and Co.'s embroidery cotton No. 50; No. 40 for the edges.

This cravat is worked on fine muslin, embroidered upon both ends in raised satin stitch; the scalloped edge is worked in button-hole stitch; the bouquet in the centre is worked in appliqué satin stitch – that is, the leaves of the rose and the foliage are worked separately on muslin; they are then cut out and worked in

88. Cravat End in Embroidery.

appliqué (see Nos. 48 and 51) upon the cravat, as seen in the illustration.

Sandwich Case

Materials: Strip of grey kid; strip of oil silk; 1 skein black silk; 1 skein red purse silk; 1 hank steel beads; steel button.

This case will be found very useful on the occasion of a journey or picnic, as it can be carried in the pocket without any inconvenience.

The case is made of a strip of grey kid, scalloped out at the edges. The words 'Bon appetit', or 'Good appetite', at will, are worked over it in overcast with black purse silk and steel beads, the scroll pattern in chain stitch with red silk. The back and front of the case are formed of the same strip, which is lined with oilskin, and to which narrow side-pieces are added to form the pocket. These pieces are lined and scalloped out in the same way as the back and front, and then the scallops of both sides are joined together, and worked round in button-hole stitch with purse silk.

The case is fastened down with a steel button.

If another colour is preferred, the sandwich case can be made of brown kid. The scroll pattern should then be worked in rich blue purse silk, and gold beads used for the letters, which should be embroidered as before in black silk. The edge may be worked in double overcast stitch in blue or black silk. A gold button must replace the steel when this alteration of colour is made.

89. Sandwich Case.

Insertion

Materials: Muslin; Messrs. Walter Evans and Co.'s embroidery cotton No. 16.

This insertion is worked in raised satin stitch between two rows of hem-stitching; a small eyelet-hole is worked in the centre of each flower.

90. Insertion.

Cravat End in Raised Embroidery

Materials: Messrs. Walter Evans and Co.'s embroidery cotton Nos. 50 and 16.

This pattern is a muslin cravat 32 inches long. The greater part of the embroidered ends is worked in satin stitch; the leaves in the bouquet of the centre are worked in raised embroidery. (See Nos. 48 and 51)

The dotted lines are raised by taking four threads of the muslin on the needle, draw it half out, wind the cotton twice round the point, holding it tightly under the thumb, draw the needle out and insert it at the place where the stitch was begun, and draw it out where the next stitch is to be worked.

91. Cravat End in Raised Embroidery.

Lady's Purse

Materials: Russia leather; blue silk; black purse silk; blue silk soutache; fine gold braid; and gold thread.

This purse is embroidered upon Russia leather; an oval-shaped medallion is cut out in the centre; a piece of blue silk is gummed on under the leather so as to show within the oval; both leather and silk are then lined with calico and stretched upon a small embroidery frame. The front and back of the purse are made all of one piece, the centre of which is the bottom; after the embroidery is completed a piece of leather is added on each side to give the necessary fullness. Four flowrets are worked over the blue silk, with black purse silk, in raised satin stitch, with a dot in gold thread for the centre. The stems are black and the leaflets gold. The inner border round the oval medallion is worked in gold braid, and the outer one in blue soutache. The network upon the leather is formed of threads of black purse silk, fastened at every crossing with a stitch of gold thread; the outer border round this network is formed entirely of gold braid. On the opposite side of the purse initials may be worked in black and gold, over the blue silk oval medallion.

The purse is lined with brown watered silk, and mounted with a clasp of gilt steel.

92. Lady's Purse.

Table-Napkin Ring

Materials: Crimson cashmere; *toile cirée*; 1 reel each of white, black, green, blue, and yellow Chinese silk.

Stretch a strip of cashmere of a bright shade of crimson over a piece of *toile cirée*, and work the pattern over it in point Russe with fine silk. The outer borders have white and black outlines, and leaflets of green silk. The stars have black and blue outlines, a yellow cross and dots. The figure between the stars is black and yellow.

93. Table-Napkin Ring.

Knife Basket

Materials: Grey American cloth; red cloth; black jet beads and bugles; red worsted braid, three-quarters of an inch wide; some strong wire; a cigar-box.

This basket is meant for holding dessert knives. It consists of a common cigar-box nine inches and two-fifths long, five inches and four-fifths wide, and two inches and one-fifth high, covered inside and out with grey American cloth, which is ornamented with embroidery worked in appliqué. The seams are made in overcast stitch. The feet consist of four pieces of strong wire three inches and two-fifths long. These pieces of wire are first covered with wool, and then with jet beads; they are then bent into loops, and fastened on at the bottom of the box by means of holes bored into it for that purpose. The feet must be fastened before covering the inside of the box. The inside of the basket is ornamented with an embroidered pattern in appliqué, which must also be worked before covering the box. The leaves are made of red cloth, the stems and veinings of black bugles. No. 95 shows the pattern in full size; the flowers and leaves are edged with light grey purse silk, over which small stitches in black silk are fastened at regular intervals. Inside the box fasten a deal board covered on both sides with American cloth, so as to divide the basket into two compartments, and fasten on to this board a handle consisting of a piece of wire seven inches long, wound round with beads. The basket is ornamented with ruches of red worsted braid; between two box pleats of the ruche a black bugle is fastened.

94 and 95. Knife Basket.

Satin Stitch Embroidery

Materials: Purse silk of two colours, in 4 shades of green and 4 shades of red or magenta for the flowers, gold twist.

This branch is embroidered with purse silk of the natural colours of the flowers and leaves, or in different shades of one colour, on silk canvas. Fuchsia blossoms are here designed, and should be worked in raised embroidery; the stamens to be worked in gold twist.

96. Fuchsia Spray.

Acacia Spray in Raised Satin Stitch Embroidery

Materials: Four shades of green purse silk for the leaves; 1 skein of brown silk; 3 shades of white or gold silk for the flowers.

This spray of acacia is worked in raised satin stitch embroidery; the flowers should be carefully shaded, and the veinings should be worked before the leaves are embroidered. The flowers may be worked gold colour, or imitate the white acacia blossom.

97. Acacia Spray.

Tobacco Pouch

Materials: Fine crimson cloth; bits of coloured and white cloth for the pattern; purse silk of various colours; white kid; brass rings; gimp cord; and silk tassels.

This pouch is cut in four pieces, two of which are given in full size; the two others must be worked after the same patterns. These patterns represent the attributes of a lover of tobacco; they are cut out of cloth and worked in appliqué over crimson cloth.

In No. 98 the outer chain stitch border is green. The knot from which the different articles are suspended is black, the cigar-case yellow in cloth appliqué, the cigars brown in satin stitch. The case is crossed by two rows of chain stitch in blue silk, and edged all round with button-hole stitch, also blue. The two pipes are of white cloth, edged round with yellow silk; the shade is imitated by long stitches of grey silk. The upper part of the pouch is of blue cloth, with a white silk edging and yellow dots; the under part of brown cloth with a black edging and a pattern worked in chain stitch with white; the three tassels are embroidered with black and yellow silk.

In No. 99 the outer border is yellow, the knots black, the small pattern at the top is of blue cloth edged with yellow; the pipes of white cloth edged with blue and shaded with grey. The bundle of cigars is of brown cloth, shaded with black silk stitches, and fastened on with double rows of chain stitch in yellow silk. The cigar-case is of light green cloth, edged with white; the Grecian pattern and dots are embroidered over it with white silk also.

To make up the pouch, cut out the four pieces and join them together by seams, which are hidden under yellow soutache; cut out also and join in the same way four pieces of white kid for the lining, and fasten it on to the crimson cloth at the top only. Sew small brass rings round the top, and pass a double piece of crimson silk cord through them. Add silk tassels of various colours at the bottom of the pouch, and at each of its four corners.

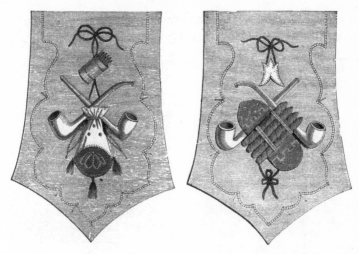

98 and 99. Tobacco Pouch.

Insertion

Materials: Linen; Messrs. Walter Evans and Co.'s embroidery cotton No. 16.

100. Insertion.

This strong and simple insertion is useful for petticoat trimmings. It is worked in button-hole stitch; the stems in overcast stitch; the circles can be filled up with lace stitches or with wheels, or the pattern may be worked upon Brussels net and the linen cut away.

Embroidery Pattern for Ornamenting Needlebooks, Workbaskets, &c.

Materials: Coloured purse silk; silk or cashmere; glacé silk; gold beads.

101. Pattern for Needlebook, &c.

This pattern is worked in French embroidery and point Russe, with coloured purse silk on silk or cashmere. The thimble, cotton, and ribbon are worked in appliqué with glacé silk. The colours are chosen according to personal taste. The thimble is ornamented with small gold beads. A bead is placed in the centre of each pair of scissors to imitate the screw.

Embroidery Pattern for Ornamenting Needlebooks, &c.

102. Pattern for Needlebook, &c.

Materials: Coloured purse silk; silk or cashmere; beads.

The shuttlecocks are worked in raised satin stitch; the feathers in point Russe; the battledores in very thickly raised double overcast; the interior is filled with a netting worked in chain stitch or dotted stitch; the flowers are worked in satin stitch and beads; the ribbon is embroidered in appliqué, with a contrasting shade of silk ribbon.

Travelling Bag

Materials: 20 inches of Java canvas; single Berlin wool of 2
shades of a pretty green; 2 shades of bronze colour and white;
floss silk – white, brown, and 2 shades of yellow; purse silk
– black, yellow, cerise, blue, and grey; steel beads; brown silk
fancy braid.

This pattern is of the ordinary shape of travelling-bags,
but it is very prettily worked. Besides the engraving showing
the bag when completed, the bouquet in the centre in full size
is given. This bouquet is also worked upon the Java canvas.
For each petal the white wool is passed several times from
one stitch of the canvas to another till the required thickness
is obtained, then 1 stitch is worked at the point with white
silk. The centres are filled up in point d'or with 2 shades of
yellow silk. The buds are made like the petals, but with 3
stitches of white silk at the point instead of 1. The leaves are
worked in 2 shades of green wool with 1 stitch of brown
silk in the centre; the stems are embroidered in overcast
with light brown wool. The scroll-pattern border round the

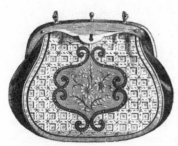

103. Travelling Bag.

104. Bouquet for Travelling Bag.

bouquet is made with brown fancy braid put on with steel beads.

The remaining space outside this border is worked in coloured purse silk. The 1st outline of the squares is worked in black silk, by inserting the needle in and out of the stitches of the canvas. When you have worked all the square thus, 12 stitches one from the other, work on either side, at one stitch's distance, the outlines of yellow silk, which are worked in back stitch, two strips of the Java canvas being covered by each stitch. Next to the inner yellow outline comes a border worked over two strips of the canvas, in slanting stitches; this border is alternately blue in one square and grey in the other. A star is embroidered in point Russe in the centre of each square; it is grey in the blue squares and blue in the grey; a steel bead is placed in the middle of each star. The small crosses between the squares are worked in cerise. The outer border of the work is composed of a piece of black soutache, edged with a tiny trefoil pattern in cerise silk. The front and back pieces of the bag are worked in the same manner. The side pieces are made of plain Java canvas. The embroidered part measures 14 inches in its widest part, and is 11 inches deep. The bag is lined with light brown silk, and made up with a steel clasp.

Embroidery Trimming for Muslin Bodices

Materials: Fine muslin; fine black silk; Messrs. Walter Evans and Co.'s embroidery cotton No. 24.

This pattern is very easily worked, and looks very nice for a trimming. It is worked on fine white muslin; the border is worked in button-hole stitch with white cotton; these scallops are covered with loose button-hole stitch in black silk. The feather-like branches are worked likewise in black silk in herring-bone stitch. The white spots are worked in raised embroidery. The large oval openings through which a narrow ribbon velvet is drawn are worked round with button-hole stitches:

105. Trimming for Bodices.

Toilet Cushion Cover in White Embroidery

This handsome embroidery pattern is to be worked on fine muslin; if lined with coloured silk or satin it is very effective. The patterns, which are covered white dots on the illustration,

Above left: 106. Toilet Cushion Cover in White Embroidery.

Above right: 107. Wing of Bird.

Right: 108. Rose Leaf.

are worked in point d'or; the outlines of these patterns are worked in fine double overcast. The flower-leaves and wings of birds, which appear raised on the illustration on account of the dark shadows, are worked separately and sewn on at the corresponding places. No. 107 shows the wing of a bird, No. 108 a rose-leaf somewhat increased in size; the former is worked entirely in button-hole stitch, or trimmed with a ruche of coloured ribbon. This pattern may also be worked on glacé silk with purse silk.

Glove Box

Materials: 15 inches of French blue cashmere; silks of various colours. A shape in bamboo cane, painted brown and varnished.

The ornamentation of this box is both novel and tasteful. It is embroidered in coloured silks, upon light blue cashmere. Part of the embroidery pattern is given in full size. All the outlines are worked in overcast, the stitches being made rather long and slanting, and the small leaves are each composed of one stitch, as in point Russe. The leaves are alternately red and yellow upon a green stem; the scalloped outline which has no leaves is red. The pine patterns are worked in satin stitch – the centre one is green, edged with red; the side ones are pink, edged with red; the small wing-like figures are black, edged with maize; the diamond, maize, edged with black, with an outer rim of maize. In the round pattern the centre is pink; the edge red, with red and yellow leaves; the 3 outer circles are successively white, green,

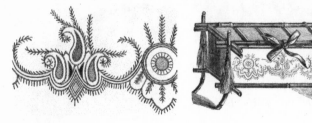

109. Pattern for Glove Box   110. Glove Box

and red; at the top the centre branch is yellow, the leaves red and yellow, the side ones are green, with the leaves pink and green.

The strip of embroidered cashmere is lined with blue silk, slipped through the bamboo-canes of the mounting, and joined together at the side by a seam. The cover is lined with plain blue cashmere, upon which initials might be embroidered at discretion. The four corners are ornamented with pretty silk tassels, of colours to match with the embroidery. To fasten the box, sew on a blue ribbon to the cover, and one to the box.

Hanging Letter Case

Materials: Crimson velvet; white satin beads; gold soutache; and fine gold bouillon.

No. 111 shows the letter case when completed in a reduced size, No. 112 the principal part of the embroidered pattern in full size.

The letter case is composed of two parts. The larger

112. Pattern for Embroidered Letter Case.

111. Hanging Letter Case.

part is 11 inches long, 8 inches wide; it is ornamented on the upper part with a pattern in gold soutache, and the word LETTERS or LETTRES embroidered in gold bouillon; underneath there is a pattern embroidered in oval white satin beads, edged round with fine white chenille; the scroll pattern is embroidered in gold bouillon.

The second part is placed over the lower part of the first, and forms the pocket which contains the letters. The centre flower is composed of 11 oval beads, edged round with white chenille; another white bead is placed in the centre, and edged with gold bouillon. The other flowers are also composed of white satin beads, edged with gold bouillon.

Embroidered Edging

Materials: Muslin; Messrs. Walter Evans and Co.'s embroidery cotton No. 24

This edging is worked in *broderie Anglaise* or overcast stitch; the edge in scallop button-hole stitch; the ovals and dots in raised satin stitch. The stems are worked in slanting overcast stitch (No. 57).

113. Embroidered Edging.

Border in Oriental Embroidery

Materials: Purse silk of the following shades: dark red, bright red, 2 shades of green, 2 of blue, 2 of yellow violet.

The four ovals placed together are worked of four contrasting colours. These ovals are composed of two rows of chain stitch. The outer row of the first oval is dark red, and the inner one bright red. Following the same arrangement, the second oval is of two shades of green; the third of two shades of blue; and the fourth of two shades of yellow. The knotted stitch in the centre is violet. The dots outside the ovals are worked in satin stitch, and are alternately red, yellow, violet, and blue. The stems are long stitches of black silk. The arabesque patterns between those formed of four ovals are worked in chain stitch with silk of two shades of brown. The colours of the ovals may be varied as much as you please, but the brown shades of the arabesque patterns should remain the same for the whole of the border.

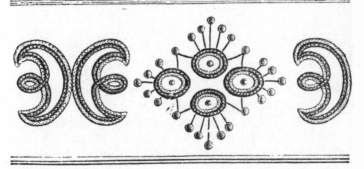

114. Border in Oriental Embroidery.

Embroidery Stars

Materials: Fine linen; Messrs. Walter Evans and Co.'s embroidery cotton No. 40.

These stars are designed for medallions, to be worked on linen collars and cuffs. No. 115 is worked in successive rows of back-stitching, round an open wheel; ladder stitch (see No. 16) is worked round this, and a raised scallop in button-hole stitch forms the edge.

No. 116 is worked in raised satin stitch; the interior of the star is filled with lace wheels.

115 and 116. Embroidery Star.

Key Bag

Materials: Grey kid; grey silk; steel-coloured glacé silk; purse silk of 5 shades of blue-green, 4 shades of brown, and silver-grey, scarlet, and white; grey silk cord; grey glacé silk ribbon.

This bag is made of grey kid, and lined with grey silk. The embroidery imitates on one side a key formed of poppies, leaves, and stems, in the upper part of which sits an owl, 'the bird of night.' The poppies are worked with blue-green purse silk in 5 shades; the plumage of the owl is worked with brown silk of 4 shades in satin stitch, the colours blending one into the other, as can be clearly seen in illustration No. 117. The eyes of the owl are embroidered in scarlet and white silk. Illustration No. 118 shows the other side of the bag, which is ornamented with steel-coloured silk appliqué figures, in the form of a Gothic lock. They are edged with fine grey silk cord. The screws of the lock are imitated in satin stitch embroidery with silver-grey silk. After having lined each part, join the two halves of the bag with a border of grey glacé silk ribbon, which must, of course, continue round the reverse. The bag is fastened by means of a loop and steel button.

117 and 118. Key Bag.

Embroidery Patterns for Trimming Cravats, Bodices, Morning Caps, &c.

Materials: Muslin or cambric; Messrs. Walter Evans and Co.'s No. 24 for lingerie, No. 12 for couvrettes.

These patterns, worked on muslin or cambric, are suitable for trimming various articles of lingerie; joined on to other squares they make pretty covers. They can also be embroidered with coloured silk, wool, or thread, on cloth, rep, or cashmere, for trimming couvrettes and toilet pincushions. The patterns should be embroidered in satin stitch and edged with chain stitch; they can also be worked in button-hole stitch. When the pattern is worked on woollen material this material must be cut away inside the leaves and spots.

119 and 120. Embroidery Pattern for Cravats, &c.

Pen-Wiper in Cloth Appliqué

Materials: 4 circles of black cloth; 1 large white, 4 small white, and 4 red circles of cloth; 4 white and 4 red stars of cloth; small black beads; gold and black purse silk; small ivory handle or figure.

This pretty little pen-wiper is covered with small circles of cloth. No. 122 is one of these circles seen in full size. There are 4 white and 4 red ones, and they are pinked out round the edge. In the centre of each red circle place a white, and in the centre of each white circle a red star, and work a cross over it with small round black beads. The border, in herring-bone stitch, is worked with gold-coloured purse silk on the red, and with black on the white cloth. The centre of the pen-wiper is covered with a circle of white cloth larger than the side ones, worked in point Russe and point Mexico in black silk. When all the circles are prepared, sew them neatly on to a round piece of red cloth, placing alternately 1 white and 1 red, so as to overlap one another, and between each a circle of black cloth, also pinked out round the edge. The work is then fastened upon a round of cardboard lined with black glazed calico, and a small handle of carved ivory, or an ivory figure, is fixed in the centre. The circles of black cloth are used to wipe the pens.

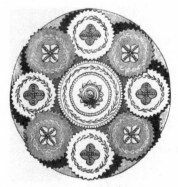

121. Pen-Wiper in Embroidery.

122. Full-Sized Circle for Pen-Wiper.

Insertion

Materials: Fine muslin; Messrs. Walter Evans and Co.'s embroidery cotton No. 30.

The flowers of this insertion are embroidered in raised satin stitch round an open eyelet hole, worked in overcast stitch the stars are worked in point Russe stitch; the four eyelet holes which surround each flower, in overcast stitch; and the edge is finished with a row of hem-stitching on each side.

123. Insertion.

Insertion

Materials: Fine muslin; Messrs. Walter Evans and Co.'s embroidery cotton No. 24.

This insertion is entirely embroidered in raised satin stitch; the dots and stems should be worked first, and the leaves afterwards. It is edged on both sides with a row of hem-stitching.

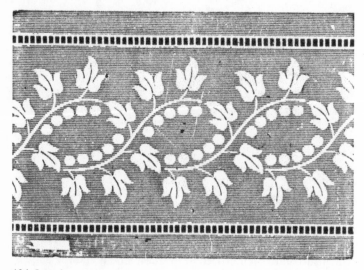

124. Insertion.

Cigar Case

Materials: Russia leather; fine silk cord; black purse silk; gold thread.

The material of this cigar case should be finely-embossed light brown Russia leather; the centre pattern to be embroidered in well-raised satin stitch with black purse silk. All the lighter outlines shown in the illustration are worked in gold thread. The border to be worked in fine silk cord of the same colour as the leather, with a network of black purse silk, stitched with gold at all the crossings. On the opposite side of the cigar case initials may be worked. The lining of light brown watered silk, or fine leather, and the mountings gilt or steel.

125. Cigar Case.

Wicker Waste Paper Basket

Materials: Basket and stand; coloured Berlin wools; cloth fringe; and glazed calico.

The basket may be of any size, but of the shape of the pattern. It rests upon two brass hooks fastened upon a stand. This stand can be made by any joiner, and should match the furniture of the room. The trimming consists of an embroidered border, lined with glazed calico, and put on round the edge; the lower part of the border is trimmed with a woollen fringe. The shades selected should correspond with the prevailing colour of the room.

126. Wicker Waste Paper Basket.

Insertion

Materials: Messrs. Walter Evans and Co.'s embroidery cotton No. 16.

The edge of this insertion is worked in raised button-hole stitch, and embroidered in sharply-pointed scallops; the dotted line is worked in raised satin stitch, as are also the flowers which compose the centre wreath; the eyelet holes are worked in overcast stitch.

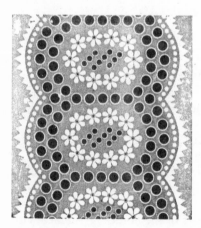

127. Insertion.

Embroidered Linen Collars

Materials: Double linen; Messrs. Walter Evans and Co.'s embroidery cotton No. 40.

These patterns are to be worked on linen taken double. No. 194 is worked in button-hole, satin, and knotted stitch (see Nos. 16, 17, 11, and 8), and point d'or with white cotton, and point Russe with black silk. No. 193 is worked entirely with white cotton in button-hole, satin, knotted ladder, and overcast stitch. (See Nos. 17, 11, 8, 16, and 3.)

128 and 129. Embroidered Linen Collar.

What-Not

Materials: Fine canvas; 3 shades of violet floss silk; 4 shades of green floss silk; sea-green wool, or floss silk; 1 skein of yellow floss silk; green chenille; cord and tassels.

This small what-not or jewel-stand is very elegant. It is meant to place upon the toilet-table. No. 130 shows the hammock when completed, No. 131 one-half of the embroidery pattern in full size; it is worked upon fine canvas. The violets are in floss silk of three shades of violet, with a raised spot worked in yellow silk in the centre, the leaves are worked in Berlin wool of various shades of green, and the stems in overcast of a light green shade. The pattern is grounded in tent stitch with sea-green silk. The hammock is composed of two sides and an under-piece cut out in cardboard, covered with the embroidered canvas outside, lined and quilted with plain green silk inside. It is edged round the top with green chenille. The mounting is composed of bamboo-canes; the hammock is fastened on to it with green silk cord, finished off with tassels.

Left: 130. What-Not in the Shape of a Hammock.

Right: 131. Pattern for What-Not.

Embroidered Handkerchief

Materials: Grass lawn or French cambric; Messrs. Walter Evans and Co.'s embroidery cotton No. 40.

This embroidery pattern is worked between the borders of a handkerchief, which may be either of French cambric or grass lawn. The design is simple, but effective, and very easy to work. If worked on fine French cambric, the handkerchief should be lightly tacked upon *toile cirée*. The rows of raised dots should be worked first, and then the graceful branches of pointed leaves in satin stitch. The plain round dots might be worked in bright red marking cotton in either of the patterns. To produce a good effect, rather fine cotton must be selected, and No. 40 will be found very effective on either lawn or cambric. For mourning wear, this pattern should be embroidered with black filoselle, or the leaves can be worked in white cotton, and the dots in filoselle.

132. Handkerchief Border.

Two Medallions for a Purse in Embroidery

Materials: Light brown Russia leather; black, scarlet, and gold silk; steel or gold clasp.

These medallions are intended to ornament a small purse, but may be employed on a variety of articles.

The raised spots of No. 133 should be worked in black silk, in satin stitch, the branched sprays in point Russe in scarlet and gold, the four largest being in scarlet and the intermediate sprays in gold silk. Medallion No. 134 is worked entirely in

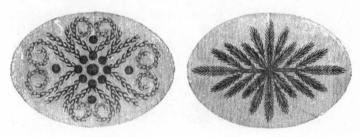

133 and 134. Medallion for a Purse in Embroidery.

point Russe, and may be embroidered in one colour, or in alternate branches of scarlet and gold, or scarlet and black.

Work-Bag

Materials: Drab cloth; small pieces of cloth of different colours; embroidery silk of different colours; scarlet satin; red silk braid; red cord; cardboard; cotton wool; and a strap of light-coloured leather.

This work-bag is made in the shape of a rolled-up plaid. The outside consists of drab cloth, trimmed with appliqué embroidery. The inside of the bag is slightly wadded and lined with red satin, which is quilted in diamonds. The seams are covered with red braid, and a leather strap completes the whole. Cut out a good pattern in paper, and then cut the satin and wadding and the drab cloth which forms the outside. After having traced the pattern on the cloth, work it with small pieces of coloured cloth in appliqué embroidery.

135. Work Bag.

The different figures are sewn over the centre partly in point Russe, partly in button-hole stitches, with embroidery silk. The stems in the middle are worked with silk in chain stitches. The colours may be chosen according to taste. Cut a pattern in cardboard, and fasten the drab cloth on it. The edge must be bordered with red satin, and the satin lining must be sewed in. The ends of the bag are likewise cut out of cardboard; the inside is wadded and lined with red satin; the outside worked in appliqué embroidery like the rest of the bag. All the seams are covered with red silk cord. The straps are fastened with a few stitches, as seen in the illustration.

Pattern for Braces

Materials: Java canvas; black silk; red wool; calico.

These braces are made of Java canvas lined with calico ornamented with embroidery in black silk and red wool, and edged on either side with loose button-hole stitch and crochet vandykes in red wool. Illustration 136 shows part of the embroidered braces, full size. Work first the embroidery of the braces, then line them with calico; work loose button-hole stitch and crochet vandykes on all the edges of the cross bands as well as at the top and bottom of these strips, and sew on the tabs for the braces between the lining and the canvas. The latter are then edged with button-hole stitch and crochet-vandykes. The vandykes are worked as follow – in one row: 1 double in 1 button-hole stitch, * 1 purl (3 chain, 1 double in the 1st), missing the next button-hole stitch under it; 1 double in the following button-hole stitch, repeat from *. The tabs are made of tape worked round with red button-hole stitch, with button-holes worked with red cotton. No. 138 shows another way of working these braces on fine ribbed piqué. Work any Berlin wool work pattern in the common cross stitch over the ribs of the piqué. For the vandyke border work in every other button-hole stitch, 2 double divided by 3 chain stitches.

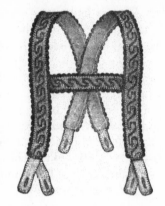

Above left: 136. Pattern for Braces.

Above right: 137. Embroidered Braces.

Left: 138. Pattern for Braces.

Embroidery Border for a Reading-Desk

Materials: White silk rep; black velvet, rep, or cloth; gold and silver brocade; gold and silver braid; silk cord and thread.

This pattern is embroidered on white silk rep with silver and gold thread, and sewn on over a black velvet, rep, or cloth centre. The dark patterns are worked in appliqué with black velvet, the two other shades in gold and silver brocade. The embroidery is worked in satin stitch with gold and silver braid, silk and cord of the same material. The border can also be worked upon the material for the centre if it is not intended to contrast with it. The pattern can also be worked entirely in silk with satin stitch. The size of the border may, of course, be increased if desired, but the third pattern in the darkest shade must, in any case, form the centre of it.

139. Embroidery Border for a Reading Desk.

Lappet or Sash End in Venetian Embroidery

Materials: Messrs. Walter Evans and Co.'s embroidery cotton No. 6 and No. 12; net and muslin.

The pattern must first be traced on muslin, which is then tacked over net. The outlines are worked in button-hole stitch, and the veinings are sewn over, using the coarse cotton for tracing; the muslin is then cut away all round the pattern.

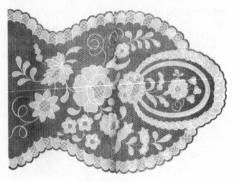

140. Lappet or Sash End in Venetian Embroidery.

Venetian Border

Materials: Messrs. Walter Evans and Co.'s embroidery cotton No. 12 and No. 16; net and muslin.

This design is elegant and effective, without there being a great deal of work in it. It is useful for tuckers for evening

141. Venetian Border.

dresses or handkerchief borders. The muslin is laid over the net, sewn neatly over, and then cut away between the pattern, leaving the net for the ground work.

Lace Insertion

Materials: Fine black sewing silk; black Brussels net.

This lace insertion is first outlined in running stitch upon the net; the leaves are then darned across the net holes; the stems are worked in overcast stitch; the dots are embroidered by darning across the circle previously outlined; the lace stitches in the centre are formed by gently enlarging the net holes

with a fine stiletto, and then sewn lightly round, the remaining holes being filled with lace stitches consisting of fine button-hole stitches, very evenly worked over the entire space surrounding the open holes.

To be effective the very finest black silk should be employed. This pattern may be worked in appliqué by placing muslin over net, sewing all the outlines in fine overcast stitch, and when finished, carefully cutting away the muslin.

142. Lace Insertion.

Slipper on Java Canvas

Materials: Light brown Java canvas; green silk; green filoselle and purse silk; green silk ribbon three-fifths of an inch wide; some wadding; 2 cork soles.

This slipper is very pretty, and easy to work. It is made of light brown Java canvas, and embroidered in point Russe with green filoselle. It is lined with green silk, and slightly quilted. The soles are of cork. The slipper is trimmed all round with a ruche of green silk ribbon three-fifths of an inch wide, pleated in double box pleats. The heel is turned down inside. No. 144 shows the pattern of the point Russe stitch nearly full size.

143. Slipper on Java Canvas.

144. Point Russe Stitch for Slipper (No. 143).

Medallions in Point Russe

Materials: Coloured filoselle, cloth, velvet, cashmere, or silk.

These medallions can be alternated for ornamenting

small covers, cushions, borders, &c. They are worked with coloured filoselle in point Russe, herring-bone stitch, coral stitch, and knotted stitch, on cloth, velvet, cashmere, or silk. The middle oval of both medallions contrasts with the colour of the ground, and must therefore be worked in appliqué on the latter with herring-bone stitch, before working the outer border. The wreath on No. 146 is worked in coral stitch; the knots, which imitate small blossoms, in knotted stitch. The choice of colours is left to the personal taste of the worker.

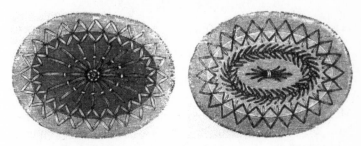

145 and 146. Medallions in Point Russe.

Butterfly for Handkerchief Corner

Materials: French lawn or cambric; fine black silk.

This butterfly is worked in the finest black silk procurable, in order more closely to imitate etching. It is worked in point Russe and scallop stitch; the dark shaded scallops are worked in button-hole scallop stitch, the stitches being taken very closely together, but not raised by the usual method of placing chain stitches beneath the button-hole stitches. The outlines and flowers are worked in point Russe, the dot in knotted stitch (see No. 8).

The initials are embroidered in raised slanting overcast stitch, and should be worked with great regularity.

147. Butterfly for Handkerchief Corner.

Pattern for a Couvrette in Appliqué

Materials: Messrs. Walter Evans and Co.'s embroidery cotton Nos. 24 and 30; cambric muslin; Brussels net; flesh-coloured silk; sewing silk of the same shade; 1 skein of a darker shade; blue silk; brown silk; gold thread.

This style of work is most effective for couvrettes or bed covers. It is worked in cambric muslin and silk, over Brussels net.

The arabesque patterns are worked in cambric muslin, the outlines are embroidered in overcast, and the material is cut away all round. The medallions are made of blue silk; the figures upon them are cut out of flesh-coloured silk, and are gummed first upon tissue-paper, then upon the blue silk; the figures are further fastened upon the medallions in overcast stitch with fine silk of a rather darker shade of flesh-colour. The scarfs are cut out of bright rose-coloured silk; the quiver and arrows and all the other attributes are worked in gold thread; the hair in fine brown silk. The edge of the blue silk medallions is worked round in button-hole stitch, but so as to be easily unripped when the couvrette has to be cleaned. A border in open ladder stitch is worked round them (see No. 16). The openings in the centre pattern are also filled in with lace stitches.

148. Couvrette in Appliqué.

149 and 150. Pattern for
Couvrette (148).

Crochet

Instructions

Cotton or thread, wool or silk, with a crochet-needle, are the materials required for working crochet. The needle, whether it be steel or bone, must be smoothly polished. The long wooden and bone crochet-needles are used for wool; for cotton and silk work short steel needles screwed into a bone handle are best. The beauty of the crochet-work depends upon the regularity of the stitches, as is the case with every other style of needlework. The stitches must be elastic, but if too loose they look as bad as if too tight. The size of the needle and that of the cotton or wool must correspond; work only with the point of the needle, and never move the stitch up and down the needle. The cotton with which you work must be of the very best quality; for borders, insertions, rosettes, imitation of guipure, use Evans's crochet cotton; for couvrettes, counterpanes, covers, &c., use knitting-cotton. All crochet-work patterns are begun on a foundation chain; there are three kinds of foundation chains – the plain foundation, the double foundation, and the purl foundation chain.

The plain foundation chain consists of chain stitches.

Crochet Hook.

Crochet

Left: 151. Plain Foundation Chain: Form a loop with the cotton or other material with which you work, take it on the needle, and hold the cotton as for knitting on the forefinger and other fingers of the left hand. The crochet-needle is held in the right hand between the thumb and forefinger, as you hold a pen in writing; hold the end of the cotton of the loop between the thumb and forefinger of the left hand, wind the cotton once round the needle by drawing the needle underneath the cotton from left to right, catch the cotton with the hook of the needle and draw it as a loop through the loop already on the needle, which is cast off the needle by this means and forms one chain stitch. The drawing the cotton through the loop is repeated until the foundation chain has acquired sufficient length. When enough chain stitches have been made, take the foundation chain between the thumb and forefinger of the left hand, so that these fingers are always close to and under the hook of the needle. Each stitch must be loose enough to let the hook of the needle pass easily through. All foundation chains are begun with a loop.

Right: 152. Double Foundation Chain: Crochet 2 chain stitches, insert the needle downwards into the left side of the 1st chain stitch, throw the cotton forward, draw it out as a loop, wind the cotton again round the needle and draw it through the two loops on the needle, * draw the cotton as a loop through the left side of the last stitch (see illustration), wind the cotton round the needle, and draw it through both loops on the needle. Repeat from * till the foundation chain is long enough.

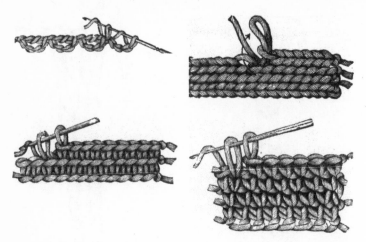

Top left: 153. Purl Foundation Chain: * Crochet 4 chain stitch, then 1 treble stitch – that is, wind the cotton round the needle, insert the needle downwards into the left side of the 1st of the 4 chain stitches, wind the cotton round the needle, draw it through the stitch, wind the cotton again round the needle, and at the same time draw the cotton through the last loop and through the stitch formed by winding the cotton round the needle. Wind the cotton once more round the needle, and draw it through the 2 remaining loops on the needle. The 4 chain stitches form a kind of scallop or purl. Repeat from *. The following crochet stitches require foundation chains like Nos. 216 and 217; they are all worked in separate rows excepting the two Nos. 222 and 234. Make a loop at the beginning of every row, as has been described (No. 216), and take it on the needle.

Top right: 154. Slip Stitch: Draw the needle through the back part of a foundation chain stitch, or in the course of the work through the back part of a stitch of the preceding row, wind the cotton round the needle, and draw through the stitch and loop on the needle. The illustration shows a number of slip stitches, the last of which is left quite loose; the arrow marks the place where the needle is to be inserted for the next stitch.

Bottom left: 155. Double Stitch: These are worked nearly like the preceding ones. Draw the cotton as a loop through the back part of a stitch, wind the cotton round the needle, and draw it through the two loops on the needle.

Bottom right: 156. Double Stitch: These double stitches are worked nearly like the preceding ones; the 1st row is worked like that of No. 220; in the following ones insert the needle into the two upper sides of a stitch of the preceding row.

Crochet

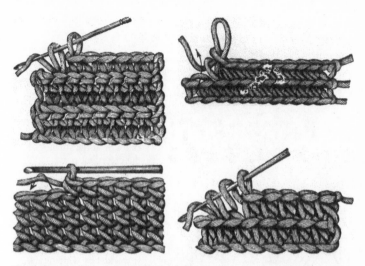

Top left: 157. Ribbed Stitch: This stitch is worked backwards and forwards – that is, the right and wrong sides are worked together, which forms the raised ribs. Insert the needle always into the back part of every stitch. Work 1 chain stitch at the end of every row, which is not worked, however, in the following row.

Top right: 158. Slanting Stitch, Double Stitch: This stitch is worked like that described in No. 155; the cotton is not wound round the needle the first time in the usual manner, but the needle is placed in the direction of the arrow, above the cotton. Draw the cotton through as a loop; the stitch is finished like the common double stitch.

Bottom left: 159. Cross Stitch: This stitch is worked like No. 157 on a foundation like No. 152, only insert the needle through the two upper sides of a stitch.

Bottom right: 160. Long Double Stitch: For this stitch wind the cotton round the needle, insert it into the back part of a stitch, draw the cotton out as a loop, wind the cotton again round the needle, and cast off together the two loops and the loop formed by winding the cotton round the needle.

161. Treble Stitch: These stitches are worked as has been described for the purl foundation chain, No. 153. The treble stitches are worked on a foundation chain or in the stitches of the preceding row.

Left: 162. Long Treble Stitch: These are worked like treble stitches, only the cotton is wound twice round the needle; the double long treble (illustration 163) is worked by winding the cotton three times round the needle. The loops formed by winding the cotton round the needle are cast off one by one with one of the loops on the needle. The two loops that remain at the end are cast off together after winding the cotton round the needle.

Below left: 163. Double Long Treble Stitch.

164–166. Cross Treble Stitch: Illustration 164 shows this stitch completed; illustrations 165 and 166 show them in the course of the work. Wind the cotton twice round the needle as for a long treble, insert the needle into the stitch in which the first half of the cross treble is to be worked, wind the cotton round the needle, draw the cotton through as a loop, wind the cotton again round the needle and cast off together with the same the loop on the needle and the loop formed by throwing the cotton forward; you have now 3 loops left on the needle, 1 of which has been formed by winding the cotton round the needle; missing these, wind the cotton again round the needle, miss the 2 next stitches of the foundation chain, and draw a loop through the third stitch. You have now 5 loops on the needle. Always cast off 2 loops at a time till only 1 loop remains on the needle. Work 2 chain stitches (if you wish to have the stitches more or less) slanting, work 1, 2, or 3 chain stitches, missing, of course, the same number of foundation chain, work 1 treble stitch, inserting the needle, as shown by the arrow on No. 231, into the 2 cross chain of the completed treble stitch.

Left: 167. Raised Spots: The grounding on which these spots are worked consists of double crochet. They are worked across 3 rows of the ground, and formed of treble stitches, the spots of one row being placed between those of the preceding. Work first 2 rows of double stitch, in the 3rd row work first 2 double stitches and then 1 spot as follows: – 1 treble, inserting the needle into both sides of 1 stitch of the first row (the preceding row is missed); the treble stitch is only completed so far that 2 loops remain on the needle; then work 2 treble stitches in the same stitch as the first, which are also only completed as far as the first treble stitch, so that after the 2nd treble there remain 3 loops and after the 3rd 4 loops on the needle (see illustration). The 4 loops are cast off together by winding the cotton once more round the needle and drawing it through. Miss under the spot the next double stitch of the preceding row; the spots are repeated at intervals of 5 stitches and in every other row.

Right: 168. Hollow Spots: The ground is worked in double crochet (illustration 155). These spots, which appear raised, consist of 5 treble stitches; they are worked in every other row at intervals of 5 stitches. For working them leave 1 loop on the needle, insert the needle between the 2 long sides of the last-worked double stitch, and work 5 treble stitches, always inserting the needle into the front part of 1 stitch of the preceding row. The first 4 treble are completed entirely without taking up the loop which was on the needle; with the fifth treble stitch only the 3 loops are cast off together by winding the cotton round the needle. Miss 1 stitch of the preceding row under the spot.

169. Open-work Spots: These spots are treble stitches divided by 2 chain; miss 2 stitches under the latter; for the rest, they are worked like the raised spots (illustration 167).

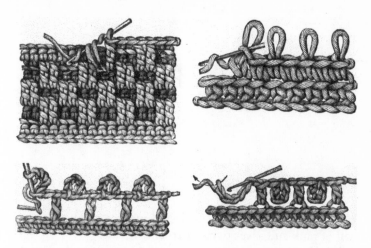

Top left: 170. Raised Treble Stitch: These stitches are long treble worked on a ribbed ground (illustration 157), and are thrown across 3 rows of the same. The raised treble are always worked on the same side of the work and in the long side of the corresponding stitch of the last row but two. After every row with treble stitch comes a row in ribbed stitch. At the beginning work 3 rows of ribbed stitch; the treble stitches begin only in the 4th row.

Top right: 171. Purl Stitch: These purl stitches imitate a lace edging perfectly well. Work 1 double, draw out the loop to a certain length (this forms the purl), take the needle out of it, insert it in the front part of the last stitch which has been worked (see illustration), wind the cotton round the needle and draw it through as a loop; 1 double, 1 purl, and so on.

Bottom left: 172. Purl Stitch Turned Upwards: Work 1 treble, then 7 chain stitch. Insert the needle into the 2nd of the 7 chain stitch downwards, so that the chain stitches form a scallop upwards (see illustration), wind the cotton round the needle and draw the cotton through; work 1 chain stitch and 1 treble in the next stitch but 3, missing 3 stitches under it.

Bottom right: 173. Purl Stitch Turned Downwards: The chain stitches form a scallop turned downwards. After having worked the 7 chain stitches take the needle out of the loop, insert it underneath the upper chain of the 2nd chain stitch, from right to left, and draw it through the loop in the direction of the arrow. Wind the cotton round the needle and cast all the loops off together. It is evident that the purl stitches may be worked at larger or smaller distances.

Crochet Patterns

Small Crochet Basket

Materials: 2 balls of closely-covered white and silver, and 1 ball of pink and silver twine; a crochet needle.

For the bottom: Make a chain of 4 stitches and unite it, work 3 long, 3 chain, and repeat three times more.

2nd round: Work 3 long into the 1st 3 chain, make 3 chain, work 3 long into the next 3 chain, make 3 chain, work 3 long into the same place, make 3 chain, and repeat.

3rd round: 3 long, 3 chain, working twice into the 3 chain of last round.

4th round: 3 long, 3 chain, increasing in every other 3rd chain by working twice into it.

5th round: Increasing in every 3rd chain, repeat.

174. Small Crochet Basket.

For the leaves: Make a chain of 32 stitches, then work a row of 1 long stitch and 1 chain stitch with the silver twine.

2nd round: Work 1 long stitch into each chain stitch in 1st row, make 1 chain stitch, repeat. (At the point, make 4 long, with a chain stitch between each), repeat on the other side of the chain, 1 long stitch and 1 chain stitch alternately.

3rd round: With pink: Work over a wire in double crochet 1 stitch into each loop, work 15 more leaves in the same way, join each leaf half way, then sew it to the centre, work a row of double crochet 1 yard in length, and twist it for the handle. This should also be crocheted over wire.

Couvrette in Crochet

Materials: Messrs. Walter Evans and Co.'s Boar's Head cotton No. 10, and steel crochet needle.

This very pretty pattern is composed of separate circles representing dahlias in raised work upon an open centre. No. 177 shows one of these large circles in full size, No. 176 one of the small circles placed in the spaces between the larger ones, No. 178 part of the border, and No. 175 the couvrette when completed, but in reduced size.

For each large circle make a chain of 20 stitches, and join it into a circle.

1st round: 30 stitches of double crochet over the circle of chain stitches.

2nd round: 36 stitches of double crochet.

3rd round: 1 double, 5 chain, miss 1. 4th round: The same as the preceding – the 1 double always on the 3rd chain.

5th round: Close double crochet; 3 stitches in 1 in the centre stitch of each loop.

6th to 12th round: The same as the 5th, close double crochet, increasing in the centre of each small scallop, which forms the 18 raised petals of the dahlia.

13th round: Here begins the open-work border round the dahlia. Work 1 double between 2 petals, taking together the 2 centre stitches, 1 double in the next, 5 chain. There will be 18 loops of 5 chain in the round.

14th to 17th round: 1 double in centre of each loop, 5 chain between. 18th round: 1 double in centre of 1st loop, 4 chain, 1 treble in next loop; in the top of this treble stitch work 3 double, with 3 chain between each; make 4 chain. Repeat the same all round, and the large circle is completed. Six of these are required.

For each small circle make a chain of 10 stitches, and join it into a round.

1st round: 16 stitches of close double crochet.

2nd round: 1 treble, 3 chain, miss 1, 8 times.

3rd round: 9 treble over each loop of chain, 1 double between. This completes 1 of the 6 small circles placed round the large ones in the centre of the couvrette. The 6 that are placed between the 5 other large circles have 1 more round, which is worked as follows: 1 treble in the centre of 1 scallop in the top of this treble stitch, 3 double, with 3 chain between each, 6 chain. Repeat the same all round.

When all the circles are completed, join them together, as seen in illustration 152, and work the border as follows:

1st round: 1 treble in one of the trefoil branches of a small circle, 8 chain, 1 treble in next trefoil, 8 chain, 1 treble in 3rd trefoil, 8 chain, 1 long treble in 4th trefoil, 10 chain, 1 long treble in 1 trefoil of a large circle, 1 treble in each of the 4 next trefoils of the large circle, 8 chain between each 8 chain, 1 long treble in the last trefoil of the large circle,10 chain. Repeat all round.

2nd round: 2 treble, with 1 chain between, in first stitch of last round, * 4 chain, miss 5, 2 treble with 1 chain between next stitch. Repeat from *.

3rd and 4th rounds: The same as the 2nd. The 2 treble always in 1 chain.

5th round: In each 1 chain, 4 treble, with 1 chain between the 2nd and 3rd, 4 chain after the 4 treble. The same all round.

6th round: The same as the 5th.

7th round: 1 treble in 1 chain, 1 trefoil in the top of the

treble, 6 chain. Repeat the same all round, which completes the couvrette.

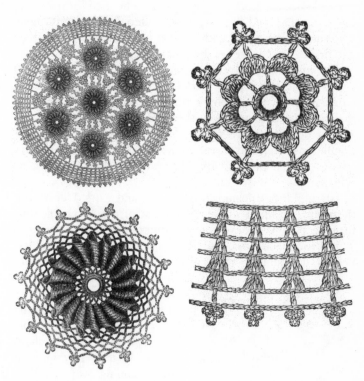

Top left: 175. Couvrette in Crochet.

Top right: 176. Showing One of the Small Circles Full Size of No. 175.

Bottom left: 177. Showing One of the Large Circles Full Size of No. 175.

Bottom right: 178. Border for Couvrettes.

Star in Crochet

Materials: Messrs. Walter Evans and Co.'s crochet cotton No. 80, or with No. 8 or 10 for couvrettes.

A number of these stars joined together will make very pretty strips of insertion. For this purpose they should be worked with fine cotton. They may also be used for trimming collars, cuffs, and cravats, the material being cut away underneath. If worked with crochet cotton No. 8 or 10, they will make nice couvrettes, bed-quilts, &c.

The star is begun by the outer circle. Make a chain of 70 stitches, and join it into a circle. * Make 10 chain, miss 3, work 1 extra long treble, 1 treble, and 1 double, inserting the needle under the chain, then 1 double worked as usual, 1 long double, 2 extra long double, miss 4, and work 1 double, inserting the needle under the 5th. Repeat 13 times from * Fasten off, and for the centre of the star work as follows:

1st round: * 10 chain, turn, miss 1 and work 1 double in the next 7 chain, 1 double in the 1st of the 10 chain, thus forming 1 loop. Repeat from * 5 times more.

2nd round: 12 double on the first loop of chain of the first branch, 1 double in the centre of the branch, 2 chain; slip

the stitch which is upon the needle in one of the stitches of the foundation chain of the outer circle, work 1 double in the first of the 2 chain last made, then 12 double in the remaining loop of chain of the branch, and 1 double at the bottom of the branch. Repeat 5 times more from *. The centre star must be joined on to the outer circle at regular distances.

179. Star in Crochet.

Crochet Silk Bag over Rings

Materials: 2 skeins each of black, blue, rose, and drab coarse purse twist; 8 skeins of the spangled silk for the top part of the bag and strings; the tassel for the bottom is made of the silks that are left; rings.

Work over a ring in double crochet, with black, 48 stitches and fasten off; this is for the centre ring. Then with the rose colour take a ring and work 24 stitches in double crochet as before, take a second ring, and work 24 double crochet over it without cutting off the silk, work over 4 more rings in the same manner, then work on the other side of the rings to correspond, join the first and last ring together, and sew in the centre ring; this completes the 1st circle. Work 12 more rounds in the same way, 3 rose colour, with drab centre, 3 blue with black, 3 drab with rose centre, 3 black with blue, join 6 circles of the alternate colours to the 1st circle, 1 to each ring, then sew the second ring to the corresponding one of the next circle, till the 6 are united; join the other 6 circles in the following manner: join one ring to the second from the one that was sewed to the 1st circle, join the next ring to the corresponding one of the next circle (which will be the one opposite to the one sewed in the 1st circle), and repeat, joining the other 5 in the same way.

For the small diamond make a chain of 5 stitches and unite it, work 4 long stitches into the circle, make 2 chain, work

180. Crochet Silk Bag.

1 single stitch to the centre of the ring missed in joining the last circle, make 2 chain, work 4 long into the circle, make 2 chain, and work a stitch of single crochet to the centre of the next ring, make 2 chain, work 4 long into the same place, make 5 chain, work 4 long into the same place, make 2 chain, and work a stitch of single crochet to the next ring, make 2 chain, and join it to the first of the long stitches; this completes the diamonds; work 5 more, joining them in the same way, then work over 12 rings, and join one on each side of every diamond; this completes the lower part of the bag. For the top part of the bag work 3 stitches of double crochet to the centre of each ring, make 5 chain, and repeat. 1st round: Work 1 long stitch, make 1 chain, miss 1 loop, and repeat. Work 12 more rounds in the same way, working the long stitch into the chain stitch of last row. Run some cord in the top of the bag to match one of the colours used, and make the tassel for the bottom from the silk that is remaining after working the crochet.

Crochet Sovereign Purse

Materials: 1 skein of black purse silk: 1 skein of coloured ditto; a few steel beads; and a steel clasp.

The open portion of this purse is worked in coloured, and the raised rose and outer border in black, silk, the latter being dotted with steel beads. A few rows of plain double crochet are worked, increasing where necessary, to make the work lie flat; then 4 rows of loops of chain in coloured silk, and then 3 rows of thick double crochet, threading the beads first on the silk, and pushing them up to the stitches when required.

The black silk must now be joined on to the centre, and the little raised piece worked in treble crochet, inserting the hook on the upper side of the stitches. Three rounds of treble are executed, and when both sides of the purse are finished they should be joined together (except where the clasp is put on) by a row of open treble, ornamented with beads. This purse is so easy to make, that it might be worked without the least difficulty from the illustration.

181. Crochet Sovereign Purse.

Stars in Crochet

Materials: Messrs. Walter Evans and Co.'s crochet cotton No. 8 or 20.

This pattern can be used for a couvrette or pincushion cover, according to the size of the cotton with which it is worked.

Each star is begun in the centre by a chain of 8 stitches. In the 1st stitch work 1 treble, * 4 chain, 1 treble in this same 1st stitch, repeat from * 3 times more, 4 chain, 1 slip stitch in the 4th of the 8 chain. You have thus formed 8 rays, joined to the 1st stitch. Now work (without cutting the cotton) the branches, which are begun from the centre.

1st branch. – 1st round: 18 chain, 1 treble in the 13th, so as to form a purl with the last 5, 2 chain, 3 treble with 2 chain between, missing 2 stitches under the 2 chain, 2 chain, 1 slip stitch in the last of the 18 chain.

2nd round: 2 double over the 1st 2 chain, 2 double with 1 purl between over the next 2 chain, 2 double over the next 2 chain, 1 purl, 7 double over the next 5 chain; then, on the other side of the branch, 1 purl, 2 double, 1 purl, 2 double, 2 double with 1 purl between, 2 double on the last 2 chain of the branch, 1 slip stitch in the stitch from which the leaf was begun, 5 double over the 4 chain of the circle. Here begins the second branch.

1st round of the 2nd leaf: 22 chain, 1 double in the last so as to form a circle.

2nd round: 1 double in each of the 10 first chain, in the next stitch work 1 double, 1 chain, 1 double to form the point, 1 double in each of the 10 remaining stitches, 1 slip stitch in the 1st stitch of the 1st round.

3rd round: 3 double, 1 purl, repeat from * twice more, then work in double crochet as far as the point, work 2 double with 1 chain between, then work the 2nd half of the branch the same as the 1st. Before beginning the next leaf, work 5 double on the chain stitches of the circle; work 6 branches, repeating alternately the 2 above explained; cut the cotton and fasten it on again to the point of one of the branches, in order to join them together by the two following rounds:

1st round: 1 double in the point of one of the leaves, * 4 chain, 1 purl under the chain; thus make 5 chain, turn the chain with the crochet to the right,

182. Stars in Crochet.

insert the needle downwards in the first chain, and make a slip stitch, 4 chain, 1 purl under, 4 chain, 1 purl under, 4 chain, 1 slip stitch in the point of the next leaf, repeat from * five times more.

2nd round: * 4 double over the nearest 4 chain; 1 purl as usual – that is, above the chain – 4 double over the next 4 chain. Now work 1 trefoil (thus: 1 chain, 1 purl, 1 chain, 1 purl, 1 chain, 1 double in the 1 double coming just before the 3 purl). 1 double on each of the next 4 chain of last round, 1 purl, 5 double, 1 trefoil, repeat five times from *.

Join the stars by a few stitches, as seen in the illustration.

Crochet Purse over Rings

Materials: 67 rings; 2 skeins each of cerise and black, and 1 of maize coarse purse silk.

Work in double crochet with maize over one ring 38 stitches; this is the centre ring for the bottom of the purse.

Then work with cerise colour over a ring 19 stitches, take another ring and work 19 stitches, repeat this till you have 6 rings, then work round the other half of each ring 19 stitches; and when the 6 are finished, join the first to the last to make a circle; sew the maize ring into the centre of it, then work over 12 rings with black in the same manner, and place them outside the cerise circle. Then work over 16 rings with maize colour, and join them beyond the black, but not to lie flat down; they are to stand up to form the sides of the purse. Work over 16 rings with cerise, and these you can join one to each of the former rounds in working the second half of the crochet, as it will save the sewing. Work over 16 rings in black, and join them in the same manner to the cerise. For the edge, with cerise, work into the centre stitch of the ring a stitch of double crochet, make 5 chain, work into the stitch joining the 8 rings an extra long stitch, make 5 chain, repeat. Then work 4 rounds of single open crochet.

6th round: * Work a stitch of double crochet and 1 chain alternately, missing 1 loop between each 4 times, then work a long stitch, make 1 chain, work into the next loop 1 long stitch, make 2 chain, work another long stitch into the same place, make 1 chain, work a long stitch into the next loop, repeat from *.

7th round: Work into the 2 chain 1 long stitch, make 2 chain, work another long stitch into the same place, * make 1 chain, work a stitch of double crochet into the 1 chain in last round, repeat from * 3 times more, miss the next 1 chain, * work a stitch of double crochet into the next 1 chain, make 1 chain, repeat from * 3 times more, then repeat from the beginning.

8th round: Join the black, work into the 2 chain 1 long stitch, make 2 chain, work another long stitch into the same place, make 2 chain, work another long stitch into the same place, make 1 chain, work a 4th long stitch into the same place, * make 1 chain, work a stitch of double crochet into the 1 chain, repeat from * 3 times more, miss the next 2 stitches of double crochet, * work a stitch of double crochet into the 1 chain, make 1 chain, repeat from * 3 times more, then repeat from the beginning.

9th round: Work into the 2 chain 1 long stitch, make 2 chain, work another long stitch into the same place, repeat the stitches of double crochet with 1 chain between, as in last round, then repeat from the beginning. 10th and 11th rounds the same as the 9th. Add a tassel at the bottom, and strings run into the last row of open crochet complete the purse.

183. Crochet Purse Over Rings.

Crochet Brioche Cushion

Materials: 10 skeins of 12-thread fleecy, of six shades of red (these should be most of the darker shades); 2 skeins of white ditto; 1 skein of white filoselle.

Make a chain of 196 stitches with the darkest shade of red wool, and join it into a circle. Work 1 round of raised spots thus: Turn the wool 5 times round the needle, insert the needle in 1 chain, and draw it through all the loops, then work 1 slip stitch, insert the needle in the next stitch, work 1 double, and begin a fresh spot. Continue in the same way all round.

2nd round: Divide the round into 7 parts; work 12 spots with the 3rd shade of red, always working 1 double between each spot, and taking care to place them between those of preceding round: after 12 spots, work 1 double, then 12 more, and so on.

3rd round: 3rd shade of red, 11 spots, 1 double.

4th round: 4th shade, 10 spots, 3 double.

5th round: 5th shade, 9 spots, 5 double.

6th round: Same shade, 8 spots, 7 double.

7th round: 5th shade, 7 spots, 9 double.

8th round: Same shade, 6 spots, 11 double.

9th round: Same shade, 5 spots, 13 double.

10th round: 6th shade, 4 spots, 15 double.

11th round: Same shade, 3 spots, 17 double.

184. Crochet Brioche
Cushion.

12th round: Same shade, 2 spots, 19 double.

13th round: Same shade, 1 spot, 21 double. The pattern of raised spots being now completed, continue to work with the lightest shade of red in double stitches, decreasing once above each pattern, so as to close up the circle gradually. The white flowers are worked over the plain part of the cushion with white wool, and silk for the petals, and a black dot in the centre. The cushion is stuffed with horsehair and lined with glazed calico. A round of thick pasteboard is stitched in at the bottom, to make it stand firmer.

Daisy Pattern for a Crochet Couvrette

Materials: For a large couvrette, Messrs. Walter Evans and Co.'s Boar's Head cotton No. 8; for pincushion covers, mats, and such-like small articles, Boar's Head cotton No. 16 or 20.

A pattern of this description is most useful, as it can be converted to so many purposes. Counterpanes, couvrettes of every description, mats, pincushions, and a thousand other things can all be arranged from the design.

Each circle is made separately, and joined to the others, as the last row is crocheted. Begin in the centre; make 8 chain, insert the needle in the first, and make * a long treble stitch, then make 3 chain, repeat 4 times from *, always inserting the needle in the 1st chain stitch, join the last chain to the 5th of the 1st 8 chain to close the round.

2nd round: Work 1 double crochet, * 9 chain, turn, work a slip stitch in each of the 9 chain; work round the stem thus made in close crochet, working 3 stitches in 1 to turn at the point; miss 1 stitch of preceding row, work 2 double crochet, and repeat from * 5 times more, making 6 petals in all.

3rd round: Work at the back of the last row, behind the petals; make 1 petal between each petal in last row, 1 double crochet at the back of each, and cut the cotton at the end of the round.

4th round: 2 double crochet at the point of each of the 12 petals, 5 chain between each petal.

5th round: 2 treble, 5 chain, repeat.

6th and last round: 1 double crochet in the centre of the 1st 5 chain, *

5 chain, 1 treble in the centre of the next 5 chain, 5 chain, 1 slip stitch in the top of the treble stitch, 6 chain, 1 slip stitch in the same place, 5 chain, a 3rd slip stitch in the same place, 5 chain, 1 double crochet in the centre of the next 5 chain, repeat from * to the end of the round. There should be 12 trefoil patterns in the round.

For the couvrette join the circles together, as shown in the illustration, in working the last round. As many circles can be added as may be required for the couvrette.

185. Daisy Pattern for a Crochet Couvrettes.

Crochet Lace

Materials: Messrs. Walter Evans and Co.'s crochet cotton No. 40 or 60.

This lace produces a very good effect when worked with fine cotton. Make a sufficiently long foundation chain, and work the 1st row entirely in double stitch.

2nd row: * 1 treble in the next stitch, 1 chain, miss 1 stitch under it; repeat from *.

3rd row: 1 long treble in the 3rd stitch of the preceding row,

* 3 purl (each consisting of 5 chain, 1 double, in the 1st of the same), 1 long treble in the same stitch of the preceding row, 1 purl, miss 3, 3 double in the 3 following stitches, 1 purl, miss 3 stitches, 1 long treble in the 4th stitch; repeat from *.

4th row: * 3 double in the middle of the next 3 purl of the preceding row, 1 purl, 2 long treble divided by 3 purl in the middle of the 3 next double in the preceding row, 1 purl; repeat from *.

5th row: * 2 long treble, divided by 3 purl in the middle of the next 3 double of the preceding row, 1 purl, 3 double in the middle of the next 3 purl of the preceding row, 1 purl; repeat from *. Repeat the 4th and 5th rows alternately till the border is wide enough.

186. Crochet Lace.

Crochet Border

Material: Messrs. Walter Evans and Co.'s crochet cotton No. 12, 16, 24, or 40.

This border is suitable for a great variety of purposes, according to the size of the cotton employed; in coarse cotton it will make a trimming for couvrettes and berceaunette covers; with fine cotton it can be used for children's clothes, small curtains, &c. Make a sufficiently long foundation chain, and work the 1st row: * 2 treble divided by 3 chain in the 1st foundation chain stitch, miss 3; repeat from *.

2nd row: * In the 1st scallop of the preceding row, 1 double, 5 treble, 1 double, then 1 chain, 1 purl (4 chain, 1 slip stitch in the 1st of the four), 1 chain, miss under these the next chain stitch scallop; repeat from *.

3rd row: 1 treble in the chain stitch on either side of the purl in the preceding row, 5 chain.

4th row: * 2 double divided by 7 chain in the two first treble of the preceding row (insert the needle underneath the upper parts of the stitch), 10 chain, 1 slip stitch in the 5th of these 10 stitches so as to form a loop, 4 chain, repeat from *.

5th row: * 1 slip in the middle stitch of the scallop formed by 7 chain in the preceding row, 4 treble, 3 chain, 5 treble, 3 chain, 4 treble, all these 13 stitches in the loop of the preceding row, so as to form a clover-leaf pattern; repeat from *, but fasten the 4th treble with a slip stitch on the 10th treble of the preceding figure.

6th row: In the first and last stitch of the 5 middle treble of the clover-leaf 1 double, 7 chain between, 7th row: * 1 double in the 2nd chain stitch of the scallop which is above the 5 middle treble of the clover-leaf, 2 chain, 1 purl (5 chain, 1 slip stitch in the 1st), 2 chain, 1 double in the next chain stitch of the same scallop, 2 chain, 1 purl, 2 chain, miss one chain of the scallop, 1 double, 2 chain, 1 purl, 2 chain, 1 double in the next chain stitch, 3 chain. 1 double in the middle stitch of the following scallop, 3 chain, repeat from *.

187. Crochet Border.

Crochet Border

Materials: Messrs. Walter Evans and Co.'s crochet cotton No. 24, 40, or 60, according to the article for which it is required.

On a sufficiently long foundation chain work the 1st row: 1 double in each chain stitch.

2nd row: Alternately 1 double, 7 chain, miss under the latter 3 stitches of the preceding row.

3rd row: 1 treble in each double of the preceding row, 1 double in the middle stitch of each scallop, 2 chain between.

4th row: 1 double on each double of the preceding row, 1 treble on each treble, 3 chain between.

5th row: 1 double on each treble of the preceding row, 3 chain between.

6th row: 1 double in each stitch of the preceding row.

7th row: * 1 treble in the 1st stitch of the preceding row, 4 chain, miss 1, 3 treble in the following 3 stitches, miss 3 stitches, 3 treble in the following 3 stitches, 4 chain, miss 1 stitch, 1 treble, 3 chain, miss 4; repeat from *.

8th row: Repeat regularly 8 treble in the scallop formed of 4 chain in the preceding row, 1 double in the middle of the following 3 chain.

9th row: * 1 double in the 4th treble of the preceding row, 2 treble, 1 long treble in next treble but 2, 2 long treble in each of the 2 following treble, 1 long treble, 2 treble in the next treble, 1 double in the next treble but 2, 3 chain, 1 purl (4 chain, 1 slip), 3 chain stitch; repeat from *.

10th row: * 1 double in the 4th treble of the preceding row, 2 chain, 1 purl, 2 chain, miss 2 under them, 1 double, 2 chain, 1 purl, 2 chain, 1 double in the next chain but 1 of the next scallop, 2 chain, 1 purl, 2 chain, 1 double in the 2 chain stitch after the purl of the preceding row, 2 chain, 1 purl, 2 chain; repeat from *.

11th row: In each scallop of the preceding row 2 double (they must meet on either side of the purl); they are divided alternately by 5 chain, and by a scallop formed of 2 chain, 1 purl, and 2 chain, only in the chain stitch scallops which join the two treble figures work no double, but 2 chain, 1 purl, 2 chain.

188. Crochet Border.

Wicker Arm Chair, Covered with Crochet

Material: Berlin wool in two colours.

The seat and back of this arm-chair are covered with two round couvrettes, worked in crochet with Berlin wool of two colours. They are fastened on the chair with woollen braid, finishing off with tassels of the same colour. Begin each couvrette in the centre with a foundation chain of 6 stitches, with the lightest wool; join them into a circle, and work the 1st round in the following manner: 12 double.

2nd round: * 3 chain, 1 double, in the next stitch of the 1st round, inserting the needle in the upper part of the stitch; repeat from * 11 times more; at the end of this round work 1 slip stitch in the 1st chain of this round. We shall not repeat any more the repetitions from * to the end of the round.

3rd round: * 4 chain, 1 double, in the next scallop of the preceding round; at the end of the round 4 chain.

4th round: 4 double in each scallop of the preceding round.

5th round: Begin to work with the darker wool and crochet slip stitch, inserting the needle in the front chain of the stitches of the 4th round.

The 6th round is worked once more with light wool, and consists entirely of double stitch, worked by inserting the needle at the back of the stitches of the 4th round, so that the slip stitches appear raised on the right side of the work, and form a round of chain stitches. The middle part of the couvrette is then finished. Illustration 192 shows it in full size.

7th round: * 2 chain, missing 1 stitch of the preceding round under them, 1 double.

8th round: * 3 chain, 1 double, in the next scallop of the preceding round.

9th round: 3 double in each scallop.

10th round, like the 5th;

11th round, like the 6th;

12th, 13th, 14th, 15th, and 16th rounds, like the 7th – 11th;

17th – 19th rounds like the 7th – 9th.

20th round: Alternately 1 treble with the light wool, 1 treble with the dark; but every treble stitch must be cast off with the wool of the colour of the next stitch; that is, a light treble stitch with the dark wool, and a dark treble stitch with the light wool. Now and then crochet 2 treble stitches in one stitch of the preceding round, so that the couvrette remains perfectly flat.

21st round: 1 double in every stitch.

The 22nd – 31st rounds consist of a double repetition of the 7th – 11th rounds.

The 32nd and 33rd rounds are made in open work like the 7th and 8th rounds.

The 34th round is worked in treble stitches like the 20th round. Then work the outer border. It consists of chain stitch scallops which are worked alternately with dark and light wool. Illustration No. 191 shows a part of the border with the treble round in full size. Work from it with the light wool 1 double on 1 light treble stitch of the preceding round, 5 chain, 1 double, on the next light treble, throw the wool off the needle and let it hang over the right side of the work; crochet with the dark wool 1 double on the treble stitch between the 2 double of this round, leave the wool on the right side of the work; 5 chain, 1 double, on the next dark treble. Take the needle again out of the loop, draw the wool on to the right side, and work the next chain stitch scallop again with the light wool.

Instead of this border, pattern No. 190 may be worked. It consists of 3 rounds to be worked after the 34th round of the couvrette.

1st round of the border: With dark wool, * 1 double in 1 stitch, of the 34th round; 1 double, 3 treble, 1 double, in the next stitch; repeat from *.

2nd round: With the light wool, * 1 treble, inserting the needle in the next treble stitch of the 34th round, thus working over the double stitch between the spots of the preceding round; 1 chain.

3rd round * 3 double in each chain stitch of the preceding round. To work the 2nd of these 3 double, insert the needle at the same time in the upper part of the middle treble of the 1st round.

4th round: Dark wool, * 1 double in each double of the preceding round, miss 1, and work 3 treble in the next stitch but one; the last of these 3 treble is cast off with light wool, miss 1, and continue to work with the light wool 1 double in the next stitch but one, miss 1, 3 treble in the next stitch, cast off the last with the dark wool, miss 1; repeat from *.

189. Wicker Arm Chair, Covered with Crochet.

190. Pattern for Arm Chair Border.

191. Border for Arm Chair (189).

192. Couvrette for Arm Chair (189).

Crochet Insertions

Material: Messrs. Walter Evans and Co.'s crochet cotton No. 30, 40, or 60.

These insertions are worked with crochet cotton of sizes which depend upon the use you wish to make of them. The insertion seen in illustration 193 is worked the long way in 8 rows. Make a sufficiently long foundation chain, and work the 1st row as follows: 1 slip stitch in the 1st stitch of the foundation, * 5 chain, miss 3, 1 double in the next stitch but 3, repeat from *.

2nd row: 1 slip stitch in the middle of the 1st 5 chain, * 3 chain, 1 slip stitch in the middle stitch of the next 5 chain, repeat from *.

3rd row: 1 treble in the 1st stitch, * 1 leaf worked as follows: 6 chain, then without noticing the loop left on the needle 1 long treble in the 2nd and 1 in the 1st of the 6 chain; these stitches are not cast off separately, but together with the loop left on the needle. Then 5 chain, miss 7, 1 treble in the 8th stitch, repeat from *.

4th row: 1 double in the 1st of the 5 chain, * 8 chain, 1 double in the 1st of the next 5 chain, repeat from *.

5th row: * 1 leaf as in the 3rd row, 1 double in the double stitch of the preceding row, 5 chain, repeat from *.

6th row: 1 treble in the point of the 1st leaf, * 7 chain, 1 treble in the point of the next leaf, repeat from *.

7th and 8th rows: Like the 1st and 2nd.

The insertion seen in illustration 194 is worked in 6 rows, and is begun in the centre on a foundation chain sufficiently long not to be worked too tight.

1st row: 4 double in the 1st 4 stitches, * 4 double divided in the same way on the other side of the foundation chain, inserting the needle in the 1st row into the 2 chain. Illustration 195 shows an insertion which imitates darned netting; it is worked on a grounding imitating netting with raised figures. The grounding consists of 9 rows. Work on a sufficiently long foundation chain the 1st row as follows: 1 cross treble in the 1st and 3rd stitch, * 2 chain, missing

2 stitches under them, 1 cross treble in the 6th and 8th stitch, repeat from *.

2nd row: 1 double in the 1st stitch, * 9 chain, miss 4 under them, 1 double in the 5th stitch, repeat from *.

3rd to 8th rows: 1 double in the middle stitch of every chain stitch scallop, 4 chain between.

9th row: Like the 1st. Work from the illustration square patterns on this grounding, consisting each of 4 leaves; for these leaves carry on the cotton taken double in double windings from 1 double stitch to another, so as to have 4 threads lying close to each other; darn these as can be seen in the illustration, with single cotton.

193–195. Crochet Insertion.

Crochet Lace

Material: Messrs. Walter Evans and Co.'s crochet cotton No. 30.

A particular kind of purl makes this border look very like guipure lace. Begin with a foundation chain worked in the following manner: * 3 chain, the last of them forms 1 purl; this is made by drawing out a long loop on the needle, taking the needle out of the loop, inserting it in the chain stitch before the last one, drawing the cotton through it, and continuing to work so that the loop out of which the needle has been drawn forms 1 purl. All the purl must be equally long; to do this more easily the loop may be kept on the needle till a chain stitch has been worked in that which comes just before the purl, continue the foundation chain, and repeat from *.

1st row: 1 long double in the 1st stitch of the foundation, * 1 chain, 1 slip stitch in the nearest purl of the foundation chain; repeat from *.

2nd row: 1 double in the 1st stitch, * 1 purl, 1 chain, missing 1 stitch under it; 1 slip stitch in the slip stitch of the preceding row; repeat from *.

3rd row: Like the 1st.

4th row: 1 double in the 1st stitch, * 1 purl, 5 chain, 1 purl, 1 chain, missing 5 stitches under them; 1 double in the 6th stitch; repeat from *.

5th row: 1 long double in the 1st stitch, 3 chain, 1 purl, 1 chain, * 1 double in the middle of the next 5 chain of the preceding row, 1 purl, 5 chain, 1 purl, 1 chain; repeat from *.

6th to 9th rows: Alternately like the 4th and 5th rows.

10th row: 1 double in the 1st stitch, * 6 chain, 1 double long treble (throw the cotton 3 times round the needle) in the 1st of these chain stitches; the stitch is only completed so far as still to leave 2 loops on the needle; 1 double long treble in the same chain stitch. This stitch is cast off so as to leave in all 3 loops, and the cotton over the needle; these loops are cast off together by drawing the cotton once through them. This forms 1 leaf, or one-half of the bell-shaped patterns. 3 purl, 1 chain, 1 leaf like the preceding one, 1 slip stitch in the 1st of the first 6 chain stitches; the other half of the pattern is then completed; 1 purl, 5 chain, 1 purl, 1 chain, 1 double in the middle stitch of the next scallop of the preceding row, 1 purl, 5 chain, 1 purl, 1 chain, 1 double in the middle stitch of the following scallop 11th row: 1 slip stitch in the next purl of the preceding row, 1 purl, 2 chain, 1 slip stitch in the next purl of the preceding row, 1 purl, 2 chain, 1 slip stitch in the following purl, 1 purl (the 3 purl which are worked on the 3 purl of the bell-shaped pattern are made in this row and in the following one as follows: Crochet 1 chain after the slip stitch, leave it for 1 purl, and work the next chain stitch in the slip stitch), 1 purl, 5 chain, 1 purl, 1 chain, 1 double in the middle stitch of the following scallop, 1 purl, 3 chain, 1 purl, 1 chain. 12th row: 3 purl on the next 3 purl of the preceding row, 3 chain between, 1 purl, 3 chain, 1 purl, 1 chain, 1 double in the middle stitch of the next 5 chain stitches, 1 bell-shaped pattern like those of the 10th row, 1 purl, 3 chain, 1 purl, 1 chain.

196. Crochet Lace.

Crochet D'Oyleys in Imitation of Point Lace

D'Oyley No. 1

Material: Messrs. Walter Evans and Co.'s Boar's Head cotton No. 20.

Pattern No. 1. – Make a chain of 8 stitches, unite it. Round 1: * 1 double crochet, 9 chain, repeat from * 7 times more, 1 double crochet, unite it to the 1st stitch. Round 2: 3 single crochet up the 3 1st of the chain in last row, *, 5 long into the loop of 9 chain, 1 chain, repeat from *. Round 3: 1 long into the 1 chain in last round, 9 chain, repeat. Round 4: 11 double crochet into the 9 chain in last round, repeat. Round 5: 1 double crochet, 5 chain, miss 1 loop, repeat. Round 6: 1 double crochet into the 5 chain, 5 chain, repeat. Round 7: The same as 6th.

No. 2. – Make a chain of 6 stitches, and unite it. Round 1: * 1 double crochet, 4 chain, repeat from * 5 times more. Round 2: Into the 4 chain 1 double crochet, 4 long, and 1 double crochet, repeat. Round 3: 1 double crochet over the double crochet in 1st round, 6 chain, repeat. Round 4: Into the 6 chain in last round 1 double crochet, 6 long, 1 double crochet, repeat. Round 5: 1 double crochet over the one in 3rd round, 8 chain, repeat. Round 6: Into the 8 chain 1 double crochet, 8 long, 1 double crochet, repeat. Round 7: 1 double crochet over the 1 in 5th round, 10 chain, repeat. Round 8: Into the 10 chain 1 double crochet, 10 long, 1 double crochet, repeat. Round 9: 1 double crochet over the 1 in 7th round, 12 chain, repeat. Round 10: Into the 12 chain 1 double crochet, 12 long, 1 double crochet, repeat. Round 11: 1 double crochet over the 1 in 9th round, 14 chain, repeat. Round 12: Into the 14 chain 1 double crochet, 14 long, 1 double crochet, repeat. Round 13: 1 double crochet over the 1 in 11th round, 14 chain, repeat. Work 3 patterns of No. 2 for this d'oyley.

197. D'Oyley No. 1.

No. 3. – Make a chain of 12 stitches, and unite it. Into the circle 1 double crochet, *, 2 long, 3 chain, repeat from * twice more, 2 double long, 4 chain, 2 double long, * 3 chain, 2 long, repeat from * twice more, 1 double crochet, 7 chain. Repeat from the beginning. In working the 2nd pattern, join it to the 1st with the 2nd 3 chain, work 3 leaves in this manner, then make only 3 chain, and work a 4th leaf without joining it to the 3rd, make 3 chain after 4th leaf, and work a stitch of double crochet into last 7 chain, make 3 chain. Work a 5th leaf, and join it to the 4th as before, 3 chain, 1 double crochet into the next 7 chain, 3 chain. Work a 6th leaf in the same way, and join it; but make no chain stitch after the 6th leaf. Work 3 patterns of No. 3 for this d'oyley.

No. 4. – The same as No. 3, only work 4 leaves instead of 6, 2 on each side. Work 3 patterns of No. 4 for this d'oyley.

No. 5. – Work the 3 1st leaves of No. 3 This is not repeated in this d'oyley.

No. 6. – Make a chain of 15 stitches, and unite it. Work into the circle 1 double crochet, 7 long, 6 double, 6 long, 5 chain, 6 double long, 7 long, 1 double crochet, 7 chain, joining the 7th long stitch to the corresponding stitch in 1st leaf, 3 chain. Work the 3rd leaf the same as the 1st without joining it to the 2nd, 3 chain, 1 double crochet into the 7 chain, 3 chain, work a 4th leaf, and join it to the 3rd, 3 chain, and join it to the 1st stitch of double crochet at the beginning of the 1st leaf. This pattern is not repeated in this d'oyley.

No. 7. – Tie a round of cotton about this size O. Round 1: 20 double crochet into the round. Round 2: 2 double crochet into successive loops, work 2 into 3rd loop, repeat. Round 3: 1 double crochet into every loop. Round 4: 1 double crochet, 5 chain, miss 2 loops, repeat. Round 5: Into the 5 chain in last round 2 long, 5 chain, 2 more long stitches into the same place, 2 chain, repeat. Round 6: Into the 5 chain 1 double crochet, 6 long, 1 double crochet, 5 chain, repeat. This pattern is not repeated in this d'oyley.

No. 8. – Make a chain of 10 stitches, and unite it. Round I: 28 double long into the circle. Round 2: 2 double crochet between each long in last round. Round 3: 1 long, 2 chain, miss 1 loop, repeat. Round 4: 3 long into the 2 chain, 1 chain, repeat. Round 5: 1 double crochet into the 1 chain in last round, 5 chain, repeat. This pattern is not repeated in this d'oyley.

No. 9. – 1st row: Make a chain of 30 stitches, work 1 long stitch into the 6th, *, 3 chain stitches, miss 3 loops, 1 long into the next, repeat from * to the end of the row. 2nd row: 11 chain, *, 1 double crochet on the other side of the chain into the centre one of the 3 between the long stitch, 1 chain, turn, and work into the 11 chain 3 double crochet and 9 long, 11 chain, repeat from * 7 times more, work into the chain stitches at the end 3 loops of 11 chain with the double crochet and long stitch as before, then work the other half of the pattern to correspond. 3rd row: Into the space between the long stitches 5 double crochet, 2 chain, repeat. This pattern is not repeated in this d'oyley.

No. 10. – Make a chain of 8 stitches, and unite it. Round 1: Into the circle 24 double long, with 1 chain between each. Round 2: 2 double crochet into the 1 chain in last round, repeat. Round 3: 1 long, 2 chain, miss 1 loop, repeat. Round 4: 1 double crochet into the 2 chain in last round, 5 chain, repeat. This pattern is not repeated in this d'oyley.

No. 11. – Make a chain of 7 stitches, and unite it. Round 1: 20 long into the circle. Round 2: 1 double crochet into every loop. Round 3: 1 double crochet, 6 chain, miss 2 loops, repeat. Round 4: 1 double crochet into the 6 chain, 7 chain, repeat. Round 5: 10 double crochet into the 7 chain, repeat. Round 6: 1 long, 2 long into the next loop, repeat. Round 7: 1 double crochet, 5 chain, miss 3 loops, repeat. This pattern is not repeated in this d'oyley.

No. 12. – Make a chain of 21 stitches, and unite it. Round 1: 30 double crochet into the circle. Round 2: *, 21 chain, join it to the 18th, work into the circle 1 double crochet, 2 long, 3 chain, 2 long, 5 chain, 2 long, 7 chain, 2 long, 5 chain, 2 long, 3 chain, 2 long and 1 double crochet, 1 single crochet into the 1st double crochet, 3 chain, 4 double crochet into the 3 chain, 2 chain, 6 double crochet into the 5 chain, 2 chain, 4 double crochet into the 7 chain, 3 chain, 4 double crochet into the same place, 2 chain, 6 double crochet into the 5 chain, 2 chain, 4 double crochet into the 3 chain, 3 chain, 1 single crochet into the stitches of double crochet at the end, 3 single crochet down the 3 for the stem, 9 single crochet into successive loops round the circle, repeat from * twice more. This pattern is not repeated in this d'oyley.

No. 13. – *, make 9 chain stitches, turn, 1 double crochet into each loop, repeat from * twice more, then work round both sides of these 3 points 1 double crochet, 3 chain, miss 1 loop at the top of each point, work twice into the same loop, then 5 chain, 1 double crochet into each end, unite the 5th to the last of the centre point of 9. This pattern is not repeated in this d'oyley.

No. 14. – Round 1: * make a chain of 13 stitches, and unite it, repeat from * 4 more times. Round 2: 1 double crochet into 6 successive loops, 3 stitches into the 7th, 1 into each of the next 6 loops, repeat. Round 3: 1 double crochet, 7 chain, 1 double crochet into the centre 1 of the 3 in last, 7 chain, miss 6, repeat. Round 4: 1 double crochet, 3 chain, miss 1 loop, repeat. This pattern is not repeated.

No. 15. – *, make a chain of 19 stitches, unite it, 3 long into successive loops, 3 double long, 2 long, 1 double crochet, 5 chain, 1 double crochet into the next loop, 7 chain, 1 double crochet into the same place, 5 chain, work into successive loops 1 double crochet, 2 long, 3 double long, 3 long, unite the last to the first, 9 chain, repeat from * once more, then 5 double crochet into the 5 1st of the 9 chain, 7 chain, 1 double crochet into each, and 1 into each of the 4 remaining of the 9 chain. This pattern is not repeated in this d'oyley.

No. 16. – Make a chain of 11 stitches, *, work into successive loops 2 double crochet, 7 long, 2 double crochet, 2 more double crochet into the same loop as the last, repeat from * once, make a chain of 24 stitches, unite to the 20th, work into the circle, *, 1 long, 3 chain, 1 long, repeat from * 12 times, work into the 3 chain 1 long, 3 chain, work another long into the same place, repeat, join the last with 1 single crochet to the last of the 24 chain, 2 double crochet over the 2 of the leaf, 7 long into successive loops, 4 double long into successive loops, 4 long into the next loop, and 1 long into the next. This pattern is not repeated. When all these pieces are done, join them as shown in the engraving, sewing them firmly together with the same cotton, then work an edging round in the following manner: 1st row: 1 double long into the 4 chain at the point of the leaf of No. 4 pattern, 7 chain, 1 double long into the 2nd 3 chain in the same leaf, 8 chain, 1 double long into the 1st 3 chain of the 2nd leaf of the same pattern, 15 chain, 1 long into the 4 chain of No. 6 pattern, 15 chain, 1 long into the 4 chain of the next leaf in the same pattern, 12 chain, 1 long into the 3rd 5 chain from the join of the 11th pattern, 6 chain, 1 single crochet into the 2nd 5 chain from the long stitch, 9 chain, 1 single crochet into the 3rd 5 chain from the last, 6 chain, 1 long into the 2nd 5 chain from the last, 12 chain, work into the 2nd 5 chain from the join of the 7th pattern 1 long, 8 chain, 1 double crochet into the next 5 chain, 9 chain, 1 long into the next 5 chain, 8 chain, 1 double crochet in the 1st 3 chain from the join of 4th pattern, 11 chain, 1 double crochet into the 1st 3 chain of the 2nd leaf of the same pattern, 6 chain, 1 double crochet into the last 3 chain of the same leaf, 4 chain, 1 double crochet into the 3 chain of No. 5 pattern, 6 chain, 1 long into the 7 chain between the leaves of the same pattern, 10 chain, 1 long into the next 7 chain, 6 chain, 1 long into the 1st 3 chain of the 3rd leaf of the same pattern, 12 chain, 1 single crochet into the 3rd 5 of double crochet from the join of 9th pattern, 8 chain, 1 single crochet into the centre of the 2nd 5 double crochet from the last, 11 chain, 1 single crochet into the 2nd 5 of double crochet from the last, 12 chain, 1 double crochet into the 7 chain of 15th pattern, 7 chain, 1 double crochet into the 6th long stitch of the same leaf, 11 chain, 1 double crochet into the end of the stem of 15th pattern, 8 chain, 1 double long into the 1st 3 chain of the 4th pattern, 4 chain, 1 double long into the last 3 chain of the same leaf, 9 chain, 1 double long into the 2nd 3 chain of the 2nd leaf, 12 chain, 1 long into the 3rd 3 chain of No. 16 pattern, 8 chain, 1 long into the 2nd 3 chain of the same pattern from the last, 12 chain, 1 long into the 3rd 5 chain from the join of the 10th pattern, 10 chain, 1 long into the 3rd 5 chain from the last, 12 chain, 1 double crochet into the centre of the 7 of double crochet in 12th pattern, 12 chain, 1 long into the 5 double crochet of same pattern, 8 chain, 1 double crochet into the 3 chain in centre of same leaf, 9 chain, 1 long into the 3rd 5 chain from the join of the 8th pattern, 8 chain, 1 single crochet into the 3rd 5 chain from the last, 10 chain, 1 double long into the 3rd 5 chain from the stitch of single, 13 chain, and join it to the double long stitch at the beginning of the row. 2nd row: *, 12 chain, and unite it, 1 chain to cross, and on the other side into the circle 1 double crochet, 2 long, 3 chain, 2 long, 3 chain, 2 double long, 4 chain, then work down the other side to correspond, 8 double crochet into successive loops of the foundation, repeat from *, joining the leaves in the 1st 3 chain.

D'Oyley No. 2

Material: Messrs. Walter Evans and Co.'s Boar's Head cotton No. 20.

Pattern No. 1. – Make a chain of 4 stitches, and unite it. Round 1: 2 double crochet into each loop. Round 2: 2 double crochet into each loop. Round 3: 1 double crochet, 2 double crochet into the next loop, repeat. Round 4: 1 double crochet into each loop. Round 5: 1 double crochet, 5 chain, miss 2

198. D'Oyley No. 2.

loops, repeat. Round 6: 9 double crochet into the 5 chain, repeat. Round 7: 9 double crochet into successive loops, beginning on the 5th of the 9 in last round, 5 chain, 1 single crochet into the last double crochet, and repeat. Round 8: 1 double crochet into the centre one of the 9 in last round, 11 chain, repeat. Round 9: 15 double crochet into the 11 chain in last round, repeat.

Round 10: 15 double crochet into successive loops, beginning on the 8th of the 15 in last round, 5 chain, 1 single crochet into the last double crochet, repeat. Round 11: 1 double crochet into the centre one of the 15 in last round, 17 chain, repeat. Round 12: 21 double crochet into the 17 chain in last round.

No. 2. – Make a chain of 7 stitches, and unite it. Round 1: *, 7 chain, 1 double crochet into the circle, repeat from * twice more. Round 2: 12 long into the 7 chain, repeat. Round 3: 2 long into each loop. Round 4: 1 long, 2 chain, miss 2 loops, repeat. Round 5: 2 long into the 2 chain in last round, 1 chain, repeat. Round 6: 1 double crochet into the 1 chain, 5 chain, repeat.

No. 3. – Make a chain of 14 stitches, and unite it. Round 1: Into the circle 1 double crochet, 7 long, 6 double long, 4 chain, 6 double long, 7 long, 1 double crochet. Round 2: 1 double crochet into every loop. Round 3: 2 chain, miss 1 loop, 1 long and repeat, 4 long at the point, finish with a single stitch, 3 chain, and repeat this once more.

No. 4. – Make a chain of 13 stitches, and unite it, chain of 15 and unite it, chain of 13 and unite it, work 6 double crochet into successive loops, beginning on the 1st of the 1st loop of 13, 3 into the next loop, and 1 into each of the 6 next, 1 double crochet into each of the 1st 7 of the loop of 15, 3 into the next, 1 into each of the next 7, 1 double crochet into each of the 6 1st of the next loop of 13, 3 into the next, 1 into each of the next 6. 2nd row: 1 double crochet, 3 chain, miss 1 loop, repeat.

No. 5. – Make a chain of 13 stitches, and unite it. Round 1: Into the circle 3 double crochet, 3 long, 3 double long, 5 treble long, 3 double long, 3 long, 3 double crochet. Round 2: 1 double crochet into each of the 9 1st loops, 2 into each of the 2 next, and 3 into the next, 2 into each of the 2 next, and 1 into each of the 9 next. Round 3: 1 long, *, 3 chain, 1 long into the next loop, repeat from * at the end, unite the last to the 1st stitch, 9 chain, repeat from the beginning; in uniting the last stitch of the 2nd leaf, take up the centre stitch of the 9 chain with it, make 5 chain, and work a 3rd leaf in the same manner; in uniting the last stitch of the 3rd leaf, take up the last of the 5 chain with it, make 9 chain, turn, and work 1 double crochet into each, join the last to the last of the 5 and 9 chain stitch.

No. 6. – Make a chain of 6 stitches, and unite it. Round 1: 1 double crochet into 1 loop, 5 chain, repeat 5 times more. Round 2: Into the 5 chain 1 double crochet, 3 long, 1 double crochet, repeat. Round 3: 1 double crochet over the 1st double crochet in last round, 7 chain, repeat. Round 4: Into the 7 chain in last round 2 double crochet, 7 long, 2 double crochet, and repeat. Round 5: 1 double crochet into the 1st double crochet in last round, 11 chain, repeat. Round 6: Into the 11 chain in last round 3 double crochet, 9 long, 3 more double crochet, repeat.

No. 7. – 1st row: Make a chain of 20 stitches. 1 long into the 15th, *, 2 chain, miss 2 loops, 1 long into the next, repeat from * to the end of the row. 2nd row: Turn, into the 2 chain 1 double crochet, 2 long, 1 double crochet, repeat this to the end, then into the 5 chain 1 double crochet, 2 long, 1 double long, 2 long, 1 double crochet, work the other side to correspond. 3rd row: 1 double crochet into the 1st double crochet in last row, 7 chain, and repeat to the point, 7 chain, 1 double crochet into the double long, work the other side to correspond. 4th row: Into the 7 chain 4 double crochet,

3 chain, 1 single into the last double crochet, 4 more double crochet into the same place, repeat.

No. 8. – 1st row: 1 chain of 7 stitches, 1 double crochet into each of the 6 1st, 3 stitches into the 7th, work on the other side of the chain to correspond. 2nd row: 1 double crochet, 3 chain, miss 1 loop, repeat. 3rd row: 5 double crochet into the 3 chain, repeat.

No. 9. – The same as No. 3 in the 1st d'oyley, only 5 leaves instead of 6, 2 on each side, and 1 at the end; 2 of these will be required for this d'oyley.

No. 10. – Work the 2 1st leaves of No. 4 in the 1st d'oyley; 3 of these will be required for this d'oyley.

No. 11. – Work only 1 leaf of No. 4 in the 1st d'oyley. This is not to be repeated in this d'oyley.

No. 12. – The same as No. 4 in 1st d'oyley.

No. 13. – The same as No. 5.

No. 14. – The same as No. 8 in 1st d'oyley.

No. 15. – The same as No. 10.

No. 16. – The same as No. 11 in the 1st d'oyley.

No. 17. – The same as No. 2 in 1st d'oyley; 2 of these will be required.

No. 18. – The same as No 6 in 1st d'oyley; 2 of these will be required. When all these pieces are done, sew them firmly together, and work the edging round in the following manner: 1 double crochet into the 1st 4 chain of 9th pattern, 9 chain, 1 double crochet into the last 3 chain of same leaf, 4 chain, 1 double crochet into the 1st 3 chain of 2nd leaf, 10 chain, 1 double crochet in the 4 chain of same leaf, 8 chain, 1 long into the 4th of the 5 chain, from the joining of 15th pattern, 4 chain, 1 double crochet into the 2nd 5 chain, 4 chain, 1 long into the 2nd 5 chain from the last, 12 chain, 1 long into the last 3 chain of 10th pattern, 3 chain, 1 double crochet into the 4 chain of same leaf, 9 chain, 1 double crochet into the 4 chain of 2nd leaf, 12 chain, 1 long into the 1st double crochet from the join of No. 6 pattern, 9 chain, 1 long into the next stitch of double crochet after the long stitch, 16 chain, 1 long into the 3rd 5 chain from the join of 14th pattern, 8 chain, 1 double crochet into the 3rd 5 chain from the long stitch, 9 chain, 1 long into the 3rd 5 chain from the stitch of double crochet, 9 chain, 1 long into the 1st 3 chain of 10th pattern, 8 chain, 1 double crochet into the 4 chain of same leaf, 12 chain, 1 double crochet into the 4 chain of 15th pattern, 8 chain, 1 double crochet into the last 3 chain of same leaf, 9 chain, 1 long into the 1st 14 chain from the join of 17th pattern, 10 chain, 1 long into the next 14 chain of same pattern, 14 chain, 1 long into the 4th 5 chain from the join of 16th pattern, 6 chain, 1 double crochet into the 2nd 5 chain from last, 6 chain, 1 long into the 2nd 5 chain from last, 12 chain, 1 double crochet into the 1st 4 chain of 9th pattern, 8 chain, 1 double crochet into the last 3 chain of same leaf, 4 chain, 1 double crochet into the 1st 3 chain of 2nd leaf, 5 chain, 1 double crochet into the last 3 chain of 2nd leaf, 6 chain, 1 double crochet into the last 3 chain of 10th pattern, 8 chain, 1 double crochet into the 7 chain of same pattern, 6 chain, 1 double crochet into the 1st 3 chain of 2nd leaf, 11 chain, 1 double crochet into the 4 chain of 11th pattern, 9 chain, 1 double crochet into the last 3 chain of same pattern, 8 chain, 1 long into the centre 3 chain of 1st leaf of 12th pattern, 7 chain, 1 double crochet into the 1st 3 chain of 2nd leaf same pattern, 7 chain, 1 double crochet into the 4 chain of same leaf, 10 chain, 1 long into the 5th 3 chain from the join of the 3rd pattern, 4 chain, 1 double crochet into the 2nd 3 chain, 4 chain, 1 long into the 2nd 3 chain of same pattern, 8 chain, 1 long into the 1st 14 chain from join of 17th pattern, 12 chain, 1 long into the next 14 chain of same pattern, 10 chain, and unite. 2nd row: The same edging as to 1st d'oyley.

D'Oyley No. 3

Material: Messrs. Walter Evans and Co.'s Boar's Head cotton No. 20.

Work 2 patterns from No. 2 in 1st d'oyley, 2 patterns from No. 3 in same d'oyley, 1 pattern from No. 4 in same d'oyley, and 1 pattern from No. 5, 2 patterns from No. 6 in same d'oyley, 1 pattern from No. 7, 1 pattern from No. 8; and 1 from

199. D'Oyley No. 3.

No. 10 in same d'oyley, 2 patterns from No. 11 in 1st d'oyley, 1 pattern from No. 2 in 2nd d'oyley, 1 pattern from No. 3 in same d'oyley, 1 pattern from No. 9 in same d'oyley, and 2 from No. 10. Then 1 pattern in the following manner: Round 1: Make a chain stitch of 12 stitches, 1 double crochet, 10 long into successive loops, 1 double crochet, 1 double crochet at the point, and work down the other side to correspond. Round 2: 2 long into each loop. Round 3: 4 chain, miss 2 loops, 1 double crochet into the next, repeat. Round 4: 1 double crochet into the 1st 4 chain of 3rd round, 5 chain, repeat. Work 1 pattern in this way, 1 chain of 14, 1 double crochet into each, 5 chain, 1 double crochet into the last double crochet, turn, 6 double crochet into the circle, with 3 chain between each, into each 3 chain, 5 long, turn, 1 double crochet between each of the 5 long, with 6 chain between each double crochet, turn, into the 1st double crochet 1 long, 2 chain, 1 double long, 2 chain, 1 treble long, 2 chain, 1 double long, 2 chain, 1 long all into the same place, 1 double crochet into the 6 chain. Repeat this 5 times more, then work down the 7 of 14, 7 long, and 7 of single crochet. The edging to be the same as in the former d'oyleys. The 1st round of the edging takes up so much space to write, that we think it better to leave it to the judgment of the worker. It will be seen by the engraving when it is necessary to work a double long or long stitch, or a stitch of single or double crochet, and the number of chain stitches between must be just sufficient to make the circle perfect. The best way is to cut a round of blue paper and place them on it from the engraving, then sew them together, and tack them to the paper, and work the 1st row of the edging before removing the paper.

D'Oyley No. 4

Material: Messrs. Walter Evans and Co.'s Boar's Head cotton No. 20.

Work 3 patterns from No. 2 in 1st d'oyley, and 2 from No. 3, 1 pattern from No. 4, 1 pattern from No. 5 in 1st d'oyley, 2 patterns from No. 6, and 1 from No. 8 in same d'oyley, 1 pattern from No. 2 in 2nd d'oyley, and 1 leaf from No. 3 in 2nd d'oyley, 1 pattern from No. 11 in 2nd d'oyley, and the following pattern.

No. 1. – Make a chain of 30 stitches, turn, miss 1 loop, 29 double crochet into successive loops, turn, 1 double crochet, 1 long, 2 double long, 8 treble long into 4 loops, 8 double long, 9 long, 4 double crochet, 3 chain, work down the other side to correspond, then 1 double crochet, 3 chain, miss 1 loop, repeat all round.

No. 2. – Make a chain of 20 stitches, turn, miss 1 loop, 2 double crochet into successive loops, * 2 chain, miss two loops, 1 long into the next, repeat from * 3 times more, 2 chain, miss 2 loops, 3 double crochet into successive loops, 1 double crochet into every loop on both sides. Next round: * 5 chain, turn, miss 1 loop, 1 double crochet, 3 long, miss 2 loops of the foundation, 1 double crochet, repeat from * at the point, miss only 1 loop, work 2 patterns of this number.

No. 3. – Make a chain of 36 stitches, turn, miss 2 loops, 2 long, *, 1 chain, 3 long, repeat from * 3 times, 1 double crochet, turn, *, 4 chain, 1 double crochet into the 1st chain stitch, repeat from * 3 times, at the point make 5 chain instead of 4, work down the other side to correspond, turn, and into each of the 4 chain 1 double crochet, 7 long, and 1 double crochet, at

200. D'Oyley No. 4.

the point 10 long instead of 7, 2 double crochet down the stem, 1 chain of 28, turn, miss 12 loops, 1 single crochet, then into the circle 20 long, turn, 1 double crochet, 5 chain, miss 1 loop, repeat, turn, 1 double crochet into the 5 chain in last row, 5 chain, repeat, turn, into the 5 chain 1 double crochet, 7 chain, repeat, turn, into the 7 chain 1 double crochet, 1 long, 7 double long, 1 long, 1 double crochet, repeat, work down the stem, 1 double crochet, 1 long, 4 double long, 1 long, 4 double crochet, 1 chain of 14, turn, miss 3 loops, 10 long, 1 double crochet, 1 double crochet, turn, 1 double crochet, 3 chain, miss 1 loop, repeat, turn, into the 3 chain 1 double crochet, 5 long, 1 double crochet, repeat, work down the stem in double crochet.

No. 4. – Make a chain of 6 stitches, and unite it. Round 1: Into the circle 16 long. Round 2: 1 double crochet into each loop, 3 chain after each. Round 3: 1 double crochet into the 3 chain, 3 chain, repeat. Round 4: 4 long into the 3 chain, repeat. Round 5: 1 double crochet, make 3 chain, miss 1 loop, repeat. *, for the leaves, 1 chain of 22, turn, 4 double crochet, 1 long, 9 double long, 1 long, 1 double crochet, 1 chain to cross the stem, on the other side 1 double crochet, 1 long, 9 double long, 1 long, 4 double crochet, 2 double crochet at the point, work down the other side to correspond, 2 double crochet down the stem, 1 chain of 8, repeat from *, 1 chain of 12, and unite it to the 3 chain of the round, turn, 12 double crochet down the stem, work another leaf in the same manner, then work a stem of 8, and make another leaf the same as before, finish with a stem of 8.

No. 5. – Round 1: Make a chain of 12 stitches, and unite it, 1 double crochet, miss 3 loops, 12 chain, repeat twice more. Round 2: Into the 12 chain 2 double crochet, 13 long, 2 double crochet, repeat. Round 3: 2 double crochet into successive loops, 13 long into successive loops, 2 double crochet into successive loops, repeat. Round 4: 1 long, 5 chain, miss 3 loops, repeat. Round 5: Into the 5 chain 2 double crochet, 5 long, 2 double crochet, repeat.

No. 6. – Make a chain of 11 stitches, and unite it. Round 1: 2 double crochet into each loop. Round 2: 1 double crochet into each loop. Round 3: 2 double crochet into 1 loop, 1 into the next, repeat. Round 4: 1 long, 5 chain, miss 2 loops, repeat. Round 5: Into the 5 chain 3 double crochet, 3 chain, 1 single crochet into the last double crochet, 3 more of double crochet into the same place, 4 chain, repeat. Round 6: 1 long into the 4 chain, 7 chain, repeat. Round 7: Into the 7 chain 4 double crochet, 3 chain, 1 single crochet into the last double crochet, 4 more double crochet into the same place, 4 chain, repeat. When all these pieces are done sew them together, as shown in the engraving, and work the edging to correspond with the other d'oyleys.

D'Oyley No. 5

Materials: Messrs. Walter Evans and Co.'s Boar's Head cotton No. 20; and 1 skein of fine embroidery cotton, by the same makers.

Pattern No. 1. – Make a chain of 8 stitches, and unite it. Round 1: 1 double crochet, 7 chain, miss 1 loop, repeat 5 times more. Round 2: Into the 7 chain 11 stitches of double crochet, repeat. Round 3: 1 double crochet into the 1st of the 11, 9 chain, miss 5 loops, 1 double crochet into the next, 9 chain, repeat. Round 4: Into the 9 chain 13 double crochet, repeat. Round 5: 1 double crochet into the 1st of the 13, 7 chain, miss 3 loops, repeat. Round 6: 5 double crochet into the 7 chain, and repeat.

No. 2. – Make a chain of 8 stitches, and unite it. Round 1: 1 double crochet, 5 chain, repeat 7 times more. Round 2: 6 chain, miss the 1st, then work into successive loops 2 double crochet and 3 long, 1 double crochet into the

201. D'Oyley No. 5.

1 double crochet in 1st round, repeat. Round 3: 1 double crochet into the 1 in 1st round, 5 chain, and repeat. Round 4: 7 chain, miss the 1st, and work into successive loops 2 double crochet, 3 long, 1 double long, 1 double crochet into the 5 chain, repeat. Round 5: 1 double crochet into the 1 in the 3rd round, 5 chain, repeat. Round 6: Same as 4th. Round 7: 1 double crochet into the 1 in 5th round, 6 chain, repeat. Round 8: 8 chain, miss the 1st, and work into successive loops 2 double crochet, 3 long, 2 double long. Round 9: Same as 7th. Round 10: Same as 8th. Two of these patterns will be required for this d'oyley.

No. 3. – Make a chain of 16, and unite it. Round 1: 2 double crochet into 1 loop, 1 double crochet into the next, repeat. Round 2: 6 double crochet into successive loops, 5 chain, 1 single crochet into the last double crochet, repeat. Round 3: 1 double crochet into the 3rd of the 6, 13 chain, repeat. Round 4: 17 double crochet into the 13 chain, repeat. Round 5: 1 long and 1 chain alternately, missing 1 loop between each. Round 6: 1 double crochet into the 1 chain, 1 chain, 1 double crochet into the next chain, 5 chain, work another double crochet into the same place, 1 chain, repeat.

No. 4. – Make a chain of 14 stitches, and unite it. Round 1: 1 double crochet, 7 chain, miss 1 loop, repeat 6 times more. Round 2: 5 double crochet into the 7 chain, repeat. Round 3: 8 chain, miss the 1st, and work into successive loops 2 double crochet, 3 long, and 2 double long, 1 double crochet into the last of the 5 double crochet, repeat. Round 4: 1 double crochet at the top of the point, 4 chain, miss 1 loop, 1 double crochet into the next, 4 chain, miss 2 loops, 1 double crochet into the next, 4 chain, 1 double crochet into the 1 in last round. Work the other side of the point to correspond. Two of these patterns will be required for this d'oyley.

No. 5. – Make a chain of 8 stitches, and unite it. Round 1: 2 double crochet into each loop. Round 2: 2 double crochet into 1 loop, 1 into the next, repeat. Round 3: 8 chain, miss the 1st, and work into successive loops, 5 double crochet and 2 long, miss 1 of the last round, work 4 double crochet into successive loops, repeat 3 times more, at the end of the round work 4 more double crochet. Round 4: 1 double crochet, 3 chain, miss 1 loop, repeat all, round the 4 points and 2 stitches beyond the 4th, 7 chain, 1 double crochet into each of the 7, finish the round with 3 chain and 1 double crochet as before.

No. 6. – Make a chain of 5 stitches, and unite it. Round 1: 1 double crochet, 5 chain, repeat 4 times more. Round 2: Into the 5 chain 1 double crochet, 3 chain, repeat till 5 double crochet are done, repeat. Round 3: 1 double crochet into the 1 in 1st round, 7 chain, repeat. Round 4: Same as 2nd. Round 5: 1 double crochet into the 1 in 3rd round, 7 chain, repeat. Round 6: Same as 2nd. Round 7: Same as 5th. Round 8: Same as 2nd, only 4 chain instead of 3. Round 9: 1 double crochet into the 1 in 7th round, 8 chain, repeat. Round 10: The same as 8th, only making 5 chain instead of 4. Four of these patterns will be required for this d'oyley.

No. 7. – Make a chain of 6 stitches, and unite it. Round 1: 1 double crochet, 7 chain, miss 1 loop, repeat twice more. Round 2: Into the 7 chain 2 double crochet, 7 long, 2 double crochet, repeat. Round 3: 1 double crochet, 3 chain, miss 1 loop, repeat, 11 chain, work 2 more leaves in the same way, 1 double crochet into the 3 chain, 4 chain, repeat round 2 sides of the leaf, 3 chain, repeat the stitch of double crochet and 4 chain round 2 sides of each leaf, joining them with 3 chain. Two of these patterns will be required for this d'oyley.

No. 8. – 1st row: Make a chain of 14 stitches, miss the 1st, and work into successive loops 5 double crochet, 5 long, 3 double long, turn. 2nd row: 2 double long into each of the 3, 9 long into successive loops, 5 long into the double crochet at the point of the leaf, 9 long into successive loops, 6 double long into the next 2 loops, 9 double long into the end of the 1st row, unite the last to the first double long in 2nd row. 3rd row: 1 double crochet, 3 chain, miss 1 loop, repeat. No loop to be missed at the point, then work with the embroidery cotton a smaller leaf on it in satin stitch, raising it first with the cotton.

No. 9. – Make a chain of 10 stitches, and unite it. Round 1: 20 long into the circle. Round 2: 1 double crochet, taking both sides of the loop, 9 chain, miss 1 loop, repeat. Round 3:

Double crochet into the centre of the 9 chain, 7 chain, repeat. Round 4: Into the 7 chain of last row 1 double crochet, 1 long, 3 double long, 1 long, 1 double crochet, repeat, then work 2 patterns from No. 2 in 1st d'oyley, 1 pattern from No. 3, 2 patterns with 3 leaves from No. 3 in 1st d'oyley, 2 patterns with 2 leaves, and 1 pattern with 1 leaf, work 3 patterns from No. 6 in 1st d'oyley.

When all these patterns are done join them as shown in the engraving, and work the edging as directed in the former d'oyleys.

D'Oyley No. 6

Material: Messrs. Walter Evans and Co.'s Boar's Head cotton No. 20.

Pattern No. 1. – Make a chain of 7 stitches, and unite it. Round 1: 2 double crochet into each loop. Round 2: 2 double crochet into 1 loop, and 1 into the next, repeat. Round 3: Increase to 30 double crochet. Round 4: 4 chain, 1 single crochet into the 1st chain, 5 double crochet, and repeat 5 times more. Round 5: 1 double crochet into the centre one of the 5 in last round, 11 chain, repeat. Round 6: 1 double crochet into every loop. Round 7: 5 chain, 1 single crochet into the 1st, 12 double crochet, and repeat. Round 8: 1 double crochet into the 6th of the 12, 15 chain, repeat. Round 9: 1 double crochet into every loop. Round 10: 7 chain, miss the 1st, and work into successive loops 1 double crochet, 2 long, and 3 double long, miss 5 loops of the last round, work 1 double crochet, repeat. Round 11: 1 double crochet over the 1 in last

202. D'Oyley No. 6.

round, miss 1 loop, 1 double crochet into the next, *, 3 chain, miss 1 loop, repeat from * 4 times more, repeat from the beginning of the row.

No. 2. – Make a chain of 20 stitches, and unite it. Round 1: 30 double crochet into the circle. Round 2: 1 double crochet, 13 chain, miss 5 loops, repeat. Round 3: 17 double crochet into the 13 chain, repeat. Round 4: 1 long, 5 chain, 1 single crochet into the 2nd of the 5 chain, miss 1 loop, repeat. Four patterns of this number will be required for this d'oyley.

No. 3. – Make a chain of 8 stitches, and unite it. Round 1: 1 double crochet, 11 chain, miss 1 loop, repeat 3 times more. Round 2: Into the 11 chain, *, 3 double crochet, 5 chain, 1 single crochet into the 1st chain, repeat from * twice more, 3 more double crochet, repeat from the beginning of the row.

No. 4. – Make a chain of 6, and unite it. Round 1: 1 long, 4 chain, repeat 5 times more. Round 2: Into the 4 chain in last row 1 long, 4 chain, work another long into the same place, 2 chain, repeat. Round 3: Into the 2 chain 3 double crochet, into the 4 chain 1 double crochet, 11 chain, work another double crochet into the same place, repeat. Round 4: Into the 11 chain 3 double crochet, 5 chain, 1 single crochet into the 1st of the 5 chain, 3 double crochet, 7 chain, 1 single crochet into the 1st of the 7, 3 double crochet, 5 chain, 1 single crochet into the 1st of the 5 chain, 3 double crochet, 2 chain, 1 double crochet into the centre one of the 3 in last round, 2 chain, repeat; then work 2 patterns from No. 2 in 1st d'oyley, 1 pattern from No. 3, 2 patterns from No. 4, 3 from No. 6, and 1 each from Nos. 11, 13, and 14 in 1st d'oyley, 1 pattern from each of Nos. 3 and 4 in 2nd d'oyley, 2 patterns from No. 2 in 5th d'oyley, and 1 pattern each from Nos. 4 and 6 in the 5th d'oyley. Sew these pieces firmly together as shown in the engraving, and add the edging as before.

D'Oyley No. 7

Materials: Messrs. Walter Evans and Co.'s Boar's Head cotton No. 20; and 1 skein of their fine embroidery cotton.

203. D'Oyley No. 7.

Pattern No. 1. – Make a chain of 16 stitches and unite it. 1st round: 2 double crochet into each loop. 2nd round: 1 double crochet into each loop. 3rd round: 1 double crochet, 9 chain, miss 3 loops, repeat. 4th round: Into the 9 chain 11 double crochet. 5th round: 1 long, 2 chain, miss 2 loops, repeat. 6th round: Into the 2 chain 1 double crochet, 3 chain, 1 single crochet into the one double crochet, work another double crochet into the 2 chain, 2 double crochet into the next 2 chain, repeat. 7th round: 1 double crochet into the 1st of the 2 in last round, 13 chain, repeat. 8th round: Into the 13 chain 11 double crochet, repeat.

No. 2. – Make a chain of 13 stitches, work 1 double crochet into each, make a chain of 15 stitches, work 1 double crochet into each, make a chain of 13 stitches, 1 double crochet into each. 2nd row: 1 double crochet into the end of each of these points, then work round both sides of these points in double crochet, working twice into the end of each point. 3rd row: 3 double crochet over the 3 at the beginning of last row, *, 4 chain, single crochet into the 1st of the 4 chain, miss 1 loop, work a long stitch into the next, repeat from * all round, at the beginning and end of the 3rd point miss 2 loops instead of 1, then work a stitch of double crochet into the 1st of the 3, 6 chain, miss the 1st, work into successive loops 2 long and 3 double crochet, 1 double crochet into the last of the 3. This completes the pattern.

No. 3. – Make a chain of 8 stitches, and unite it. 1st round: 2 double crochet into each loop. 2nd round: 1 double crochet into 1 loop, 2 double crochet into the next, repeat. 3rd round: 2 double crochet into successive loops, 2 double crochet into the next, repeat. 4th round: 11 double crochet into successive loops, *, 9 chain, miss 2 loops, 1 double crochet into the next, repeat from *. 5th round: 11 double crochet over the 11 in last round, work into the 9 chain 5 double crochet, 5 chain, 1 single crochet into the 1st of the chain, 5 more double crochet into the same place, repeat. 6th round: 13 double crochet over the 11 in last round, *, 15 chain, 1 double crochet over the 1st of the 5 in last round, repeat from *. 7th round: 13 double crochet over the 13 in last round, *, work into the 15 chain 8 double crochet, 5 chain, work a stitch of single crochet into the 1st of the 5, 8 double crochet into the same place, repeat from *. This completes the pattern. Then work a circle in satin stitch on the plain part of the pattern with the Fine Embroidery Cotton. Two of these patterns will be required for this d'oyley.

No. 4. – Make a chain of 16 stitches, and unite it. * make a chain of 10 stitches, miss the 1st, and work into successive loops 3 double crochet, 3 long, and 3 double long, unite the last double long to the 4th of the 16 chain in the circle, repeat from * 3 times more, *, work in single crochet to the top of the point and down 6 stitches of the other side, then make a chain of 8 stitches, miss the 1st, work into successive loops 3 stitches of double crochet, 2 long, and 2 double long, unite the last to the 3rd of the next point, and repeat from * 3 times more. Three of these patterns will be required for this d'oyley. Work 2 patterns from No. 2 in the 1st d'oyley, work 2 patterns from No. 3 in the same d'oyley, work 1 pattern from No. 5, and 1 from No. 6 in 1st d'oyley, work 2 patterns with 1 leaf from No. 3 in 1st d'oyley, and 1 pattern with 2 leaves, work 2 patterns from No. 3 in the 5th d'oyley, and 1 pattern from No. 4 in the same d'oyley, and 1 from No. 6, work 6 patterns from No. 3 in the 6th d'oyley, and 1 pattern from No. 4 in the same d'oyley, work 1 pattern from No. 2 in 6th d'oyley. Join these pieces as before, and add the same edging.

D'Oyley No. 8

Materials: Messrs. Walter Evans and Co.'s Boar's Head cotton No. 20; and 1 skein of their fine embroidery cotton.

204. D'Oyley No. 8.

Pattern No. 1. – Make a chain of 9 stitches, work a stitch of double crochet into each of the 8 1st, work 2 into the 9th, work down the other side of the chain to correspond, and unite it. 2nd round: *, Work 1 long, make 4 chain, 1 single crochet into the 1st of the 4 chain, miss 1 loop, and repeat from *. No loop to be missed at the point. When this round is finished, make 10 chain, miss the 1st, and work into successive loops 2 long, and 7 of double crochet, then make 15 chain, unite to the 7th, and work into the circle 1 double crochet, make 5 chain, repeat 5 times more. 2nd round: Work into the 5 chain 1 double crochet, 3 long, and 1 of double crochet, repeat. 3rd round: Work 1 double crochet, make 3 chain, miss 1 loop, and repeat. Three of these patterns are required for this d'oyley.

No. 2. – Make a chain of 6 stitches. 1st round: Work 2 double crochet into each loop. 2nd round: Work 1 double crochet, make 9 chain, miss 1 loop, repeat. 3rd round: Work into the 9 chain 1 long, make 1 chain, work another 1 long into the same place, make 1 chain, work a third 1 long into the same place, make 7 chain, and repeat. 4th round: Work into the centre of 3 long 2 long, make 5 chain, work 2 more long into the same place, make 5 chain, work into the centre of the 7 chain 1 double crochet, make 3 chain, work another of double crochet into the same place, make 5 chain, and repeat. Two of these patterns will be required for this d'oyley. Work 1 pattern from No. 2 in 1st d'oyley, work 1 pattern from Nos. 3, 4, and 6, work 1 pattern with 3 leaves from No. 3 in 1st d'oyley, and 2 with only 1 leaf, work 1 pattern from each of Nos. 13 and 14 in 1st d'oyley, work 1 pattern from 2 in 5th d'oyley, and 1 from No. 4 in the same d'oyley, work

2 patterns from No. 6 in 5th d'oyley, work 3 patterns from No. 3 in 6th d'oyley, and 2 from No. 4 in the same d'oyley, work 1 pattern from No. 1 in 7th d'oyley, work 2 patterns from No. 3, and 1 pattern from No. 4 in 7th d'oyley, then sew them together as before.

D'Oyley No. 9

Material: Messrs. Walter Evans and Co.'s Boar's Head cotton No. 20.

Pattern No. 1 – Make a chain of 10 stitches, and unite it. 1st round: Work into the circle 1 long, make 3 chain, repeat 11 times more. 2nd round: Work 1 double crochet into every loop. 3rd round: *, Make 11 chain, turn, miss 1 loop, work 10 double crochet down the chain, miss 1 loop, work 7 double crochet and repeat from * 5 times more. 4th round: Work 1 double crochet, beginning on the 1st of the 10, make 5 chain, miss 3 loops, work 1 double crochet, make 5 chain, miss 3 loops, work 1 double crochet, make 5 chain, work 1 double crochet into the point, work down the other side to correspond, make 2 chain, miss 3 loops, work 1 double crochet, make 2 chain, miss 3 loops, and repeat. 5th round: Work into each of the 5 chain 1 double crochet, 5 long stitches, and 1 double crochet.

No. 2. – Make a chain of 20 stitches, and unite it. 1st round: Work a stitch of double crochet into 1 loop, work 2 double crochet into the next, repeat. 2nd round: * Work 3 double crochet, make 5 chain, work 1 single crochet into the 1st of the 5 chain, repeat from * 9 times more, work 2 double crochet. 3rd round: * Make 21 chain stitches,

205. D'Oyley No. 9.

work 1 double crochet in the centre one of the 3, turn, work 7 double crochet into the 21 chain, make 5 chain, work 1 single crochet into the 1st of the 5 chain, work 7 double crochet into the 21 chain, repeat from * 8 times more. 4th round: Work 15 double crochet into each loop of 21 chain, above the last 7 work 20 double crochet into the last loop of 21, make 5 chain, turn, work 1 single crochet into the last of the 5 chain, 7 double crochet, make 4 chain. 5th round: Work 19 double crochet, beginning on the 1st of the 7 in the 1st loop of 21 chain, * make 6 chain, turn, miss 1 loop, work into successive loops a stitch of double, 3 long, 1 double long, then miss 4 double crochet stitches, work 5 double crochet into successive loops, make 5 chain, 1 single crochet into the 1st of the 5 chain, miss 1 loop, 5 double crochet into successive loops, repeat from * 8 times more, then work 12 double crochet. Two of these patterns will be required for this d'oyley.

No. 3. – Make a chain of 8 stitches, and unite it. 1st round: Work into the circle 1 long, make 3 chain, repeat 9 times more. 2nd round: Work into the 3 chain 1 double crochet, make 17 chain, work another stitch of double crochet into the same place, make 1 chain, work 1 double crochet into the next 3 chain, make 1 chain, and repeat. 3rd round: Work into the 17 chain 20 double crochet, work 1 double crochet into the 1 chain, make 1 chain, work 1 double crochet into the next 1 chain, and repeat. 4th round: Work a stitch of double crochet into the 1 chain in last round, * work 5 double crochet into successive loops, beginning on the 1st of the 20, make 5 chain, work 1 single crochet into the 1st of the 5, repeat from * twice more, then work 5 double crochet into successive loops, and repeat from the beginning of the round. Two of these patterns will be required for this d'oyley.

No. 4. – Make 21 chain and unite it, make a chain of 27 and unite it, make a chain of 21 and unite it. 1st round: Work in the 21 chain 25 stitches of double crochet, work into the 27 chain 31 double crochet, work into the 21 chain 25 double crochet. 2nd round: Work 3 stitches of double crochet into successive loops, make 5 chain, work 1 single crochet into the 1st of the 5 chain, repeat this 6 times more, then work 3 double crochet and repeat from the beginning in the centre loop, repeat this 9 times instead of 7. Two of these are required for this d'oyley.

No. 5. – Make a chain of 44 stitches, work 1 double crochet into each, turn, make 21 chain, work 1 double crochet into the 4th chain on the other side, * make 21 chain, miss 3 loops, work 1 double crochet into the next, repeat from * 9 times more, work 1 single crochet into the end loop, work 44 double crochet into successive loops, work 15 double into the 1st loop of 21, work 4 double crochet into each loop of 21, and 15 into the end one, then * work 2 double crochet, make 3 chain, work 1 single crochet into the 1st of the 3, repeat from * all round.

Work 2 patterns from No. 2 in 1st d'oyley, 1 from No. 3, 2 with 3 leaves, and 2 with 2 leaves, from No. 3 in 1st d'oyley, 2 patterns from No. 6 in same d'oyley, and 3 patterns from No. 3 in 6th d'oyley, sew them together as shown in the engraving, and add the edging as before.

D'Oyley No. 10

Material: Messrs. Walter Evans and Co.'s Boar's Head cotton No. 20.

Pattern No. 1. – Make a chain of 19 stitches, turn, miss 5 loops, work 10 double crochet, make 3 chain, miss 3 loops, work 1 long, make 3 chain stitches, miss 3 loops, work 1 long stitch, make 3 chain stitches, work a stitch of double crochet into the last loop, then work into the 1st 3 chain on the other side, 1 double crochet, 5 long, work into the next 3 chain 4 long stitches, work 4 long stitches into the next 3 chain stitches, then work into the 5 chain at the point 8 long stitches, then work down the other side to correspond, * make 3 chain, miss 1 loop, work 1 long, make 1 chain, work 1 long stitch into the same place, make 1 chain, work another long stitch into the same place, miss 1 loop, work 1 double crochet, repeat from * 7 times more, then work into the 1st 3 chain 1 double crochet, make 1 chain, work 1 long stitch, *

206. D'Oyley No. 10.

make 1, work 1 double long stitch, repeat from * twice more, make 1 chain, work 1 long; all these stitches are worked into the same 3 chain, then work 1 double crochet into the chain stitch between the 2nd and 3rd long stitches, repeat this 7 times more; this finishes the leaf; then make 16 chain, and work a second leaf the same as 1st, then work 2 double crochet down, then make 12 chain, and work a third leaf the same as 1st, work 14 stitches down the stem, and work a 4th leaf the same as 1st, work 8 double crochet down the stem, work a 5th leaf the same as 1st, make a chain of 40 stitches, turn, and work back in double crochet.

No. 2. – Make a chain of 10 stitches, and unite it, *, work a stitch of double crochet into the circle, make 13 chain, and repeat from * five times more, then work 17 stitches into each of the 13 chain, then work 2 stitches of double crochet, beginning on the second of the 13, *, make 5 chain stitches, and work a stitch of single crochet into the 1st of the 5 chain, then work 2 stitches of double crochet, and repeat from * 5 times more; for the stem make a chain of 30 stitches, turn, * work 5 stitches of double crochet, make 5 chain, turn, and work a stitch of single crochet into the 1st, repeat from * 4 times more, then work down the other side to correspond; then work 1 pattern from No. 2 in 1st d'oyley, and 2 from No. 3, 2 with only two leaves, and 2 from No. 6 in the same d'oyley; work 1 pattern from No. 6 in 5th d'oyley, and 3 from No. 3 in 6th d'oyley; work 1 pattern from No. 2 in 9th d'oyley, and 1 from No. 3; work 3 patterns from No. 4 in the same d'oyley, sew the pieces together as before, and work the edging.

Work-Basket in Straw and Silk Crochet-Work

Materials: Straw; brown floss silk; brown ribbon, 1-1/4 inch wide; small glass beads; a piece of bamboo cane.

This basket has a cover formed of two pieces. It can be employed for many things, and is formed entirely of crochet-work with brown silk over straw. A ruche trimmed with beads and bows of brown silk ribbon form the trimming of the basket. The straws over which you crochet must be damp, so as not to be stiff. They should be of unequal length, and when you join the two ends of two straws together, try to hide the beginning with the other straws. Begin the basket in the centre of the bottom part with 46 stitches; then work 9 rounds on either side of this first row, working alternately 1 double stitch, 1 or 2 chain stitches, the double stitch in the chain stitch of the preceding round, the last round over wire.

It is necessary to increase regularly in all the rounds to keep the work flat. When you have finished the bottom begin the border of the basket, which is worked of the same piece with it, and consists of 11 rounds.

It is worked in the same way as the bottom, the first 2 rounds without increasing the number of stitches, but in the following 9 rounds increase 2 double stitches at both ends, in order that the edge may be a little wider in the upper part. In the last round add a piece of wire to the straws.

Left: 207. Work Basket in Straw and Crochet.

Right: 208. Bottom of Work Basket (207).

The cover of the basket is formed of two pieces. Begin in the middle with 28 stitches; crochet each half in rows forming a half circle, working backwards and forwards; at the beginning of each row turn the straws, and take care that the rows which are finished form a straight line. Each half of the cover requires 9 rows; the last one is worked over wire. The two halves are united at the straight sides by a brown silk ribbon 1-1/4 inch wide, which is sewed on underneath, and which forms a sort of hinge; sew on also a piece of wire covered with brown silk, so as to make the hinge stronger. Form the handle with a piece of bamboo cane 23 inches long, and covered with straws; work over it in long stitches of brown silk, and let it go down to the bottom of the basket; then sew the cover on the handle with the brown ribbon, which forms the two parts. Trim the basket with a ruche of double box pleats, ornamented with glass beads and with bows of brown silk ribbon.

Two Crochet Borders

Materials: Messrs. Walter Evans and Co.'s crochet cotton Nos. 30 and 80.

1. Crochet cotton of two sizes is used for this border (No. 30 and No. 80); it is begun in the centre by a chain of stitches of the length required.

1st row: 1 double in each stitch of the chain.

2nd row: Turn and work on the opposite side of the chain, * 1 double, 11 chain, miss 7. Repeat from *.

3rd row: * 1 double on the 1st loop of chain, 2 chain, 1 double in the centre of the 7 stitches which are under the 1st loop of chain, 2 chain, 1 double on the same loop, 5 chain. Repeat from *.

4th row: * 1 double in the centre of the 1st loop of chain, 3 chain, 1 treble in the 1st, but before you complete the treble stitch make 1 chain. Repeat from *. This row completes the upper half of the border. The lower half is worked over the 1st row of plain double crochet.

5th row: 1 double in each of the first 5 stitches, 15 chain, miss 9, 1 double, come back over the loop of chain and work 1 double in each stitch, come back again and work 6 small points, each made thus: 5 chain, 1 double in the 4th, and 1 treble in each of the 3 others, 1 double over the round scallop. When you have worked the 6 small points repeat from *, but always join the 1st point of one scallop to the last point of the next scallop. The pattern inside the scallops is worked in 2 rows with fine cotton. (See illustration.)

209. Crochet Border.

2. The border is begun above the pointed scallops, filled up with lace stitches, by making alternately 3 chain, 1 purl (i.e., 5 chain and 1 slip stitch in the 1st). When the chain is long enough, turn and work the 1st row: Alternately 7 chain, 1 double in the centre stitch between the 2 purl.

2nd row: Turn, work 1 double in the centre of the 1st loop of 7 chain, 1 chain, 1 purl, 1 chain, 1 double in the centre of next loop, and so on.

The 3rd row (which is the last) is worked on the opposite side of the chain with purl. * In each of the 8 first stitches work 1 double, make 12 chain, miss the 4 last of the 8 double just worked, and work 1 double in the 5th, come back over the loop of chain, and work 7 small points over it. For each point make 3 chain, work 1 double in the 2nd, 1 treble in the 1st of the 3 chain, 1 double upon the loop of chain. Repeat from * 6 times more.

In the following scallops always fasten the first point of one scallop to the last point of the preceding

210. Crochet Border.

scallop. When this row is completed fill up the inner part of each scallop with a network of fine thread, joining the threads at all the places where they cross each other by 2 or 3 stitches with a sewing needle.

Crochet Antimacassar

Materials: 18 reels of Messrs. Walter Evans and Co.'s Boar's Head cotton No. 10.

This pattern can be adapted for a round couvrette or a square one, and is also pretty done in silk for a sofa cushion. Make a chain of 4 stitches, and unite it.

1st round: Work into 1 loop a long stitch, make 1 chain stitch, work another long stitch into the same place, make 1 chain, repeat.

2nd round: 3 long stitches into 1 loop, make 2 chain stitches, miss 1 loop, and repeat.

3rd round: 1 double crochet into the 2 chain in last round, make 7 chain, and repeat.

4th round: Into the 7 chain 2 double crochet, 5 long stitches, and 2 more double crochet, and repeat.

5th round: 1 long stitch into the 1st double crochet in last round, make 9 chain, and repeat. 6th round: Into the 9 chain 2 double crochet, * make 4 chain, work 2 double crochet, repeat from * 3 times more, make 5 chain, work a stitch of single crochet into the 2nd of the 5, make 1 chain stitch, and repeat from the beginning of the round. 7th round: 1 long stitch into the loop formed with the 5 chain, make 12 chain, and repeat. 8th round: Into the 12 chain 2 double crochet into successive loops, make 4 chain, work 1 double crochet into each of the 2 next loops, make 1 chain, work into the 6th loop 1 double crochet, 5 long stitches, and another double crochet, make 1 chain, miss 1 loop, work 2 double crochet into successive loops, make 4 chain, work 1 double crochet into each of the 2 next, make 5 chain, and repeat. This completes the circle. 120 circles sewn together like the engraving will make a good-sized couvrette, 12 in the length, and 10 in the width. If a round couvrette is wished, work 1 circle for the centre larger than the others; this can be done by repeating the 5th and 6th rounds, then sew 8 circles round the centre one, and increase the number of circles in each row till you have made it the size you wish. For the square one, tassels are required for the end and sides; these are made by winding the cotton over a cardboard 4 inches deep about 80 times, then twist 8 threads of the cotton into a cord, cut the cotton wound on the cardboard at one end, make 2 inches of the cord into a loop and tie it firmly with the middle of the tassel, then turn it, tie a thread tightly round, about an inch below the cord, and net over the head; 40 of these tassels will be sufficient.

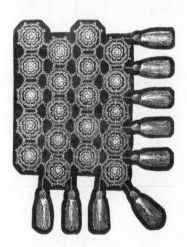

211. Crochet Antimacassar.

Crochet Insertion

Material: Messrs. Walter Evans and Co.'s crochet cotton No. 40.

The patterns of this insertion are worked in a row, and always two opposite circles at a time. Make a foundation chain of 16 stitches, join them into a circle, then work a 2nd circle consisting again of 16 chain stitches. Work round this circle 24 double stitches, and 24 double round the 1st circle; after the last stitch begin again at the 2nd circle, and work 10 chain scallops as follows: 3 double in the next 3 stitches, * 5 chain, 2 double in the next 2 stitches, repeat 8 times more, 3 double in the last 3 stitches; work in the same manner round the other circle. To get to the next pattern, work 4 slip stitches between the 2 circles in the middle of the just-completed

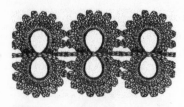

212. Crochet Insertion.

pattern, leaving the cotton under the work and drawing it through the stitch upwards through the loop on the needle; 7 chain stitches, and then 2 circles like those just described, and so on.

Tobacco Pouch in Crochet Work

Materials: Black purse silk; crimson ditto; gold thread.

The pouch is begun at the bottom, in the centre of the star.

With crimson silk make a chain of 3 stitches, and join it into a circle. Work 4 rounds of double crochet, 2 stitches in each stitch.

5th round: 2 crimson stitches, 1 gold stitch, and so on.

6th round: All gold stitches.

7th round: 2 crimson stitches, 2 gold, and so on.

8th round: All crimson stitches.

9th round: 3 crimson stitches, 2 gold, &c.

10th round: Similar to the preceding.

11th round: 4 gold stitches, 3 crimson, &c.

12th round: 4 gold stitches, 2 black stitches over the 2 centre gold stitches of preceding round, &c.

13th round: 3 gold stitches, 4 black stitches, &c.

14th round: 1 gold stitch, 6 black stitches, &c.

15th round: 3 gold stitches, 4 black stitches, &c.

16th round: 4 gold stitches, 2 black stitches, &c.

17th round: 4 gold stitches, 2 over the black stitches of preceding round, and 1 on either side, 4 crimson stitches, &c.

213. Star for Tobacco Pouch, No. 214.

18th round: 2 gold stitches over the centre ones of preceding round, 7 crimson stitches, &c.

Now work 4 plain crimson

rounds, and begin the pattern from No. 214. The centre is crimson, and the pattern is black and gold. The border round the top is of the same colours.

Complete the work by 2 rounds of open treble crochet, and 1 round of gold scallops.

In the open rounds pass a double cord of black silk, finished off with small balls of black silk gimp and gold; and on either side of the pouch fasten one of these same balls with two tassels, one crimson and one black. The pouch is lined with white kid.

214. Tobacco Pouch.

Crochet Rosettes

Material: Messrs. Walter Evans and Co.'s crochet cotton No. 4, 24, or 40.

These rosettes are suitable for trimming cuffs, collars, and bodices, or for making couvrettes, according to the size of the cotton with which they are worked.

1. Make a foundation chain of 22 chain; join them into a circle and work the 1st round; 44 double.

2nd round: * 7 chain, missing 3 stitches of the preceding round under them, 1 double; repeat 10 times more from *.

3rd round: 1 slip stitch

215. Crochet rosette.

in the first 4 stitches of the next scallop, * 5 chain, miss the last and work back on the other 4, 1 double, 1 treble, 1 long treble, 1 double long treble (throw the cotton 3 times round the needle), 1 slip stitch in the middle stitch of the next scallop; repeat 10 times more from *. Work a wheel in the centre of the rosette, which is ornamented with a circle of chain stitch, as can be seen in the illustration; take up one thread of the wheel with every other chain stitch.

2. Begin the rosette with a leaf-like pattern in the centre, and work the 1st row: * 11 chain, miss the last, work back over the following 8 stitches, 1 double, 1 treble, 2 long treble, 1 double long treble, 2 long treble, 1 treble, 1 double in the upper part of the chain stitch before the last, 1 slip stitch in the lower part

of the same stitch. The first leaf of the middle pattern is then completed; repeat 6 times more from *. Join the first and last leaves together by working 1 slip stitch in the 1st of the 11 chain stitch. 2nd round: (Fasten on the cotton afresh), 1 slip stitch in the point of each leaf, 12 chain between. 3rd round: 24 double in each scallop. The rosette is then completed.

216. Crochet Rosette.

Crochet Trimming, with Embroidered Flowers worked in Appliqué, and Velvet Ribbon

This trimming consists of 2 strips of crochet insertion, ornamented with embroidery patterns worked in appliqué, and velvet ribbon drawn through. They are worked the long way with fine crochet cotton. Begin on a sufficiently long foundation chain of stitches which can be divided by 20, and work the 1st row: 1 chain, * 5 double, on the first 5 stitches of the foundation, 1 leaf, as follows: 10 chain, without reckoning the loop left on the needle, 1 extra long treble (for which the cotton is wound 5 times round the needle) in the second of the 10 chain, a similar treble in the first, then cast off the 2 treble stitches together, wind the cotton once round the needle, and cast off the last loop with the loop left on the needle. Miss under the leaf 15 stitches of the foundation, and repeat from *.

2nd row: 5 double on the 5 double of the preceding row, inserting the needle in the whole stitches, 15 chain stitches between.

3rd row: * 5 double in the first 5 double of the preceding row, 7 chain, 1 slip stitch in every other stitch of the next scallop of the preceding row, 7 chain between, 7 chain stitches; repeat from *.

4th row: * 1 double in the middle of the 5 double of the preceding row, 3 chain, 1 slip stitch in the middle stitch of each of the 8 scallops, consisting of 7 chain in the preceding row, 3 chain between, 3 chain; repeat from *. These 2 last rows (the third and fourth) are repeated on the other side of the foundation chain.

When the 2 strips of insertion are completed, sew them together so that 2 opposite scallops meet, and ornament them with the embroidery patterns and velvet ribbon.

217. Crochet Trimming, with Embroidered Flowers Worked in Appliqué and Velvet Ribbon.

Crochet Insertion

This pretty insertion is very suitable for cerceaunette covers or pillow-cases, and should be worked with middle-sized cotton. If the insertion is used for anything but a pillowcase, omit the lower border on which the button-holes are made. Begin the insertion in the middle of one of the star-like figures, with a foundation chain of 9 stitches; join them into a circle by making 1 slip stitch, and crochet thus: * 10 chain, 1 slip stitch in the 5th of these chain; this forms 1 purl; 4 chain, 1 slip stitch in the circle, repeat from * 5 times more. Work 4 slip stitches in the next 4 chain, then crochet * in the next purl; 5 double divided by 5 chain, 4 chain, repeat 5 times from *. Fasten the thread after having fastened the last 4 chain-stitches with a slip stitch to the 1st double stitch of this round. This completes the star-like figure. Work on one side of these figures the following rows:

1st row: * 1 treble in the 2nd scallop of the four placed together, 3 chain, 1 double in the next scallop, 3 chain, 1 treble in the last of the 4 scallops, 3 chain, 1 treble in the 1st scallop of the following 4 placed together, 3 chain, 1 double in the next 2nd scallop, 3 chain, 1 treble in the 3rd scallop, 3 chain. Repeat from *.

2nd row: 3 treble in the 1st stitch of the preceding row, * miss 3 stitches, 3 treble in the 4th following stitch. Repeat from *.

3rd row: * 3 treble cast off together as one stitch on the next 3 stitches of the preceding row, 2 chain. Repeat from *.

4th row: 1 double on the next stitch of the preceding row,

* 4 chain, 1 slip stitch in the 3 double; this forms 1 purl; 3 double on the next 3 stitches of the preceding row. Repeat from *. After having worked these four rows likewise on the other side of the star figures, work over the last the following 5 rows for the button-holes:

218. Crochet Insertion.

1st row: 1 double in the next purl, * 2 chain, 1 double in the next purl. Repeat from *.

2nd row: 1 double in each stitch of the preceding row.

3rd row: Alternately 11 double, 7 chain, under which miss 7 stitches.

4th row: Like the 2nd row.

5th row; * 3 double on the next 3 double of the preceding row, 1 purl (4 chain, 1 slip stitch in the last double stitch). Repeat from *.

Crochet Insertion

Material: Messrs. Walter Evans and Co.'s crochet cotton No. 30.

This insertion is worked in our pattern with fine crochet cotton on a double foundation chain. For the outer edge work a row of purl stitches as follows: 1 double in the 1st stitch, * 1 chain, 1 purl, consisting of 5 chain, 1 slip stitch in the 1st 2 chain, 1 double in the next stitch but 2; repeat from *. The open-work centre consists of 6 rows of scallops; the 1st of these rows is worked on the other side of the foundation chain; 1 double in the middle stitch of every scallop, 5 chain between, then 1 row of slip stitches, and finally a row of purl stitches like the 1st row of the insertion. For the raised flowers, which are fastened over the grounding at unequal distances, * make a foundation chain of 10 stitches, fasten it on over the grounding from the illustration by taking the needle out of the loop, inserting it into the 1 chain of the grounding, and drawing the loop through; miss the last of the 10 chain, and work back over the others; 1 slip stitch, 1 double, 1 long double, 3 treble, 1 long double, 1 double, 1 slip

219. Crochet Insertion.

stitch, then 1 slip stitch in the 1st stitch, * 9 chain, missing 5 stitches under them, 1 double in the 6th stitch; repeat from *. Each following row consists of 1 double in the middle stitch of every scallop of the preceding row, 9 chain between. Then work the 1st row of the border on the other side of the insertion; 1 double in the 1st stitch of the foundation, inserting the needle into the back part of the stitch; repeat 8 times more from *, and the flower is completed.

Crochet Garter

Materials: Grey thread of medium size; fine red wool; fine round white elastic cord; a pearl button.

This garter is worked in close double crochet, over fine elastic cord; the border and pattern in red wool, the centre in grey thread.

Begin in the middle by a chain of 98 stitches, with red wool; take the elastic cord, which must always be stretched out a little, and work over it. Work on both sides of the foundation chain; the pattern is completed in the course of the two first rounds; the button-hole is made at the beginning of the first round; make a loop of 21 stitches, and, when you come to it, work over this loop instead of over the foundation chain. Increase the number of stitches at either end of the garter, to round it off. When the second round is completed work two plain grey rounds, then a plain red one. The last round (grey thread) is composed of alternately 1 double, 1 purl formed of 3 chain, 1 slip stitch in the first, missing 1 stitch under the 1 purl. Sew on a pearl button to correspond with the button-hole. The garter would be both more elegant and more elastic if worked entirely in silk.

220. Crochet Garter.

Crochet Trimming for a Lady's Chemise

Materials: Messrs. Walter Evans and Co.'s crochet cotton, and a needle to match.

This pattern, as can be seen in the illustration, is an imitation of old guipure lace; it is worked all in one piece for the bosom and sleeves, and is part of one of the shoulder-pieces in full size. Both strips of rosettes join at that place, and one is continued for the part round the bosom and the other for the sleeve. In the pattern there are 42 rosettes round the bosom, and 14 round each sleeve. These rosettes are fastened one to another in the course of the work. They are made in the following manner: Make a chain of 6 stitches, and join it into a ring. 1st round: 8 chain, 1 slip stitch in the 4th chain, which forms a purl (the 3 first chain are reckoned as 1 treble), 1 chain, 1 treble in the ring, * 5 chain, 1 slip stitch in the 1st to form a purl, 1 chain, 1 treble in the ring. Repeat 6 times from *. Instead of the last treble, work a slip stitch to fasten the end of the round to the 3 chain of the beginning, which thus form 1 treble.

2nd round: 9 chain (the 3 first to be reckoned as 1 treble), * 1 treble on the 1st treble of last round, 6 chain. Repeat 6 times from *. 1 slip stitch in the treble at the beginning.

3rd round: On each scallop of preceding round work 2 double, 1 purl, 2 double, 1 purl, 2 double, 1 purl, 2 double. This completes the rosette. Each rosette is fastened to the last by joining the 2 middle purl of both. In the illustration, which is full-size, the purl that are to be joined to those of another rosette are marked by a cross. The joining between the part round the bosom and the

221. Crochet Trimming for a Lady's Chemise.

sleeve is made in the same manner. The space left between 4 rosettes is filled up with a star formed of chain stitches, marked in our illustration with an asterisk. For this star make a chain of 5 stitches, the 1st of which forms the centre; slip the loop you have on the needle through one of the 8 purl that are free, make 5 chain, 1 double in the centre stitch. Repeat 7 times from *; then tie the two ends tightly, or sew them together 3 of these stars are required for each shoulder.

For the Border. – It is worked at the same time both round the bosom and sleeves. 1st round: * 1 double in the centre purl of the 1st scallop of the rosette, which we will call the first rosette; 5 chain, 1 double in the centre purl of the 2nd scallop of the same rosette, 4 chain; then work the kind of cross which comes between each rosette (see illustration). To make this cross throw the cotton 3 times round the needle, work 1 double treble in the last purl left free of the 1st rosette, keep the last loop on the needle, throw the cotton twice round it, and work a double treble in the 1st purl left free in the 2nd rosette, throw the thread twice round the needle, work 1 treble with the loop left on the needle, make 2 chain, and work 1 treble in the last double treble, which completes the cross; make 4 chain. Repeat from * at each slit on the shoulders; after the last cross make 6 chain, 1 slip stitch in the 2 purl at the end of the slit, 6 chain to come to the next space, where a cross is to be made.

2nd round: Work alternately 1 treble, 2 chain, miss 2; at the slit on the shoulders work 6 double over the 6 chain. The two rounds just explained are also worked round the upper edge, and finished round the sleeves by the following round: 1 double in one of the spaces in last round, * 6 chain, 1 double in the 2nd of the 6 chain, which forms a purl, 1 chain, 1 double on the next but one of the last round, 6 chain, 1 double in the 2nd of the 6 chain, 1 chain, 1 double in the next space. Repeat from *. On the upper edge of the bosom, between the 1st and 2nd rounds of the border, work 1 round of crosses, but throwing the cotton twice only round the needle, so that the treble stitches are not double; make 3 chain between each cross.

Knitting

Knitting though considered to be an old-fashioned art, is by no means so ancient as lacemaking. Knitting has never entirely quitted the hands of English and German ladies; indeed, among all good housewives of any civilised country, it is reckoned an indispensable accomplishment. Knitting schools have been established of late years both in Ireland and Scotland, and Her Majesty the Queen has herself set an example of this industry, as well as largely patronised the industrial knitters of Scotland. Of the rudiments of this useful art many ladies are at present ignorant; it is in the hope of being useful to these that the following instructions are offered.

To knit, two, three, four, or five needles, and either thread, cotton, silk, or wool are required.

Knitting needles are made of steel, of ivory, or of wood; the size to be used depends entirely upon the material employed, whether thread, cotton, silk, single or double wool, for knitting. As the size of the needles depends upon that of the cotton, a knitting gauge is used (see No. 222). Our readers will remark that English and foreign gauges differ very essentially; the finest

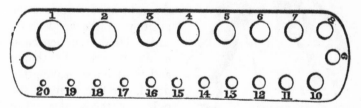

222. Knitting Gauge.

size of German needles, for example, is No. 1, which is the size of the coarsest English wooden or ivory needle. Straight knitting is usually done with two needles only for round knitting for socks, stockings, &c., three, four, and five needles are employed.

Casting On

This term is used for placing the first row or round of knitting stitches on the needles – 'casting them on' – and is done in two

223. Casting On.

ways – by 'knitting on' the stitches, or as follows:

Hold the thread between the first and second finger of the left hand, throw it over the thumb and first finger so as to form a loop, and pass the needle in the loop; throw the thread lightly round the needle, pass it through the loop, and draw up the thread; this forms the first stitch (see No. 223).

To Knit On

224. Knitting On.

Take the needle on which the stitches are cast in the left hand, and another needle in the right hand – observe the position of the hands (No. 224). Hold the left-hand needle between the thumb and third finger, leaving the first finger free to move the points of the needles. (The wonderful sense of touch in the first or index finger is so delicate, that an experienced knitter can work without ever looking at her fingers, by the help of this touch only – in fact, knitting becomes a purely mechanical labour, and as such is most useful.) Insert the point of the right-hand needle in the loop or stitch formed on the left-hand needle, bring the thread once round, turning the point of the needle in front under the stitch, bringing up the thread thrown over, which in its turn becomes a stitch, and is placed on the left-hand needle.

Simple Knitting (plain)

Pass the right-hand needle into the 1st stitch of the left-hand needle, at the back throw the thread forward, and with the first finger pass the point of the needle under the stitch in forming a fresh stitch with the thread already thrown over, as in 'knitting on,' only, instead of placing the newly-formed stitch on the left-hand needle, leave it on the right-hand needle, and let the stitch drop off the point of the left-hand needle. Continue thus until all the stitches are taken from the left to the right-hand needle, and the row is then complete.

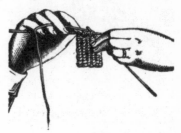

225. Plain knitting.

To Purl, Pearl, or Seam

Seaming or purling a stitch is done by taking up the stitch in front instead of at the back, throwing the thread over and knitting the stitch as in plain knitting; but before beginning to purl, the thread must be brought in front of the needle, and if a plain stitch follows, the thread is passed back after the purl stitch is made (see No. 226).

226. Purling.

To Increase

Increasing or making a stitch is done by throwing the thread once round the needle and in the next row knitting it as an ordinary stitch.

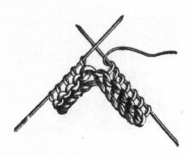

227. Increasing.

To Decrease

228. Decreasing.

This is done in two ways: firstly, taking up two stitches and knitting them together as one; secondly, by taking up a stitch without knitting it, called slipping, then by knitting the following stitch in the usual way, and then slipping the 1st (unknitted) over the 2nd (knitted) (see

No. 228). When it is necessary to decrease two stitches at once, proceed thus: Slip one, knit two stitches together, then slip the unknitted stitch over the two knitted together.

Round Knitting

To knit a round four or five needles are used; it is thus that stockings, socks, cuffs, mittens, &c., are made. To knit with four needles, cast on, say, 32 stitches upon one needle, insert a second needle in the last stitch of the first, and cast on 30 stitches; proceed in a similar way with a third needle, but casting on 28 only; when this is done, knit the two extra stitches on the first needle on to the last; this makes 30 stitches upon each needle, and completes the round.

Casting Off

Knit two stitches, and with the left-hand needle slip the first stitch over the second; continue this to the end of the row. Note. – The last knitted row, before casting off, should be knitted loosely.

To Pick up a Stitch

This is done by taking up the thread between two stitches and forming a stitch with it.

The following Designs of New Stitches can be used for a variety of work:

Peacock's Tail Pattern

Needles, wood or ivory; Messrs. Walter Evans and Co.'s knitting cotton.

Cast on a number of stitches divisible by nine, as it takes nine stitches for each pattern, and two for each border; the

229. Peacock's Tail Pattern.

border, which is in plain knitting, will not be mentioned after the first row.

1st Row. – 2 plain for border; 2 plain *, make 1, 1 plain, repeat this four times from *, make 1, 2 plain; repeat from the beginning – then 2 plain for border.

2nd Row. – 2 purl, 11 plain, 2 purl; repeat.

3rd Row. – Take 2 together, 11 plain, take 2 together; repeat.

4th Row. – Purl 2 together, purl 9, purl 2 together; repeat.

5th Row. – Take 2 together, 7 plain, take 2 together.

Begin from the 1st row. Thirteen stitches are large enough for a stripe for a sofa-cover. These stripes should be sewn together after all are finished.

Spiral Stitch

230. Spiral Stitch.

Materials: Needles, thick steel or bone; double wool.

This stitch is far more effective worked in thick wool than in cotton. It is done in stripes alternately wide and narrow. For wide stripes cast on twenty-one stitches, for narrow fifteen; this without counting the first and last stitch, the first being slipped, the last always plainly knitted.

1st Row. – Purl 3 together to end of row.

2nd Row. – Make 1, * 1 plain, make 2, repeat from * end by

making the last stitch before the plain knitted one at end of row.

Knotted Stitch

Materials: Needles, wood or ivory; double wool.

Cast on 11 stitches.

1st Row. – All plain, throwing the wool twice round the needle before each stitch.

2nd Row. – Each stitch on the needle is now composed of 3 threads of wool: knit the first plain, the second purl, the third plain; cast off the second over the third, and the first over the second; this leaves but one stitch; repeat from first row until a sufficient length is obtained. This pattern makes very pretty borders.

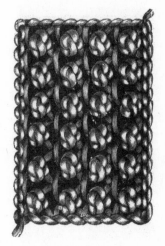

231. Knotted Stitch.

Knitted Moss Borders

Materials: Steel needles; moss wool of several shades of green.

Cast on enough stitches for double the width required, say twenty, and knit very tightly in plain knitting, row by row, until a sufficient length has been obtained. Cut off and place the strip on a sieve over a basin of boiling water, and cover it over. When it has absorbed the steam, and while wet, iron it with a box-iron. Then cut the strip down the centre, and unravel the wool on each side. The threads of wool all curling, resemble moss. They are held firmly by the selvedge of the knitting.

German Brioche Stitch

Materials: Wood or ivory needles; wool.

Cast on an even number of stitches.

All the rows are knitted as follows: Slip 1, taken as for purling, make 1, take 2 together. In the following rows the made stitch must always be slipped, the decreased stitch and the slipped stitch of the previous row knitted together.

Ordinary Brioche Stitch is made by casting on an even number of stitches, and working the rows as follows:

Make 1, slip 1, take 2 together; repeat. Note. – The made stitch and the slipped stitch of the previous row must always be knitted together, and the decreased stitch of that row slipped.

232. German Brioche Stitch.

Knitting Patterns

Knitted Sock for a Child

Materials for 1 pair: 1 ounce of single Berlin wool; 1 yard of narrow pink or blue ribbon; 2 fine steel pins.

This sock fits well, and is easy to make. It is knitted upon two pins, backwards and forwards. Cast on 22 stitches and knit 22 rows, but increase once at the end of every other row on the right side of the work, so that there are 33 stitches in the 22nd row. Now cast off 28 stitches and knit 12 rows, increasing 1 stitch at the end of every other row. Now 12 more rows, decreasing 1 stitch at the end of every other row; this forms the toe. Cast on 28 stitches on the same needle, and knit 22 rows, decreasing 1 stitch at the end of every other row, and cast off. Pick up the 68 stitches on the upper part of shoe, and knit 20 rows, alternately 2 plain and 2 purl rows, decreasing 1 stitch on each side of the 12 stitches in every other row, which forms the toe and front of sock. Knit 14 rows of 2 plain, 2 purl stitches alternately, then 3 open rows with 1 plain row between. The open rows are worked as follows: * Purl 2 together, purl 1, make 1, repeat *, 3 plain rows, 1

233. Knitted Sock.

open row, 1 plain row, and cast off. The sock is sewn together down the back of leg, centre of sole, and the point joined like a gusset to form the toe.

Knitted Pattern for Counterpanes, Berceaunette Covers, Couvrettes, Antimacassars, &c.

Materials: Messrs. Walter Evans and Co.'s knitting cotton; 5 steel knitting-needles of a corresponding size.

According to the size of the cotton employed, this beautiful square makes different articles, such as counterpanes, couvrettes, &c. &c. If worked with Evans's cotton No. 10, it will be suitable for the first-mentioned purpose. Begin the square in the centre, cast on 8 stitches, 2 on each needle; join them into a circle, and knit plain the 1st round.

2nd round: * Knit 1, throw the cotton forward, knit 1; repeat 3 times more from *.

3rd round: Plain knitting. This knitted round is repeated after every pattern round. We shall not mention this again, nor the repetition from *.

4th round: * Knit 1, throw the cotton forward, knit 1, throw the cotton forward, knit 1.

6th round: * Knit 1, throw the cotton forward, knit 3, throw the cotton forward, knit 1.

234. Knitted Pattern for Counterpanes, Berceaunette Covers, &c.

8th round: * Knit 1, throw the cotton forward, knit 5, throw the cotton forward, knit 1.

The 9th to 18th rounds are knitted in the same manner, only in every other round the number of stitches between the 2 stitches formed by throwing the cotton forward increases by 2, so that in the 18th round 15 stitches are knitted between.

20th round: * Knit 1, throw the cotton forward, knit 1, throw the cotton forward, knit 5, slip 1, knit 1, draw the slipped over the knitted stitch, knit 1, knit 2 together, knit 5, throw the cotton forward, knit 1, throw the cotton forward, knit 1.

22nd round: * Knit 1, throw the cotton forward, knit 1, throw the cotton forward, slip 1, knit 1, draw the slipped over the knitted stitch, throw the cotton forward, knit 4, slip 1, knit 1, draw the slipped over the knitted stitch, knit 1, knit 2 together, knit 4, throw the cotton forward, knit 2 together, throw the cotton forward, knit 1, throw the cotton forward, knit 1.

24th round: * Knit 1, throw the cotton forward, knit 1, throw the cotton forward, slip 1, knit 1, draw the slipped over the knitted stitch; throw the cotton forward, slip 1, knit 1, draw the slipped over the knitted stitch, throw the cotton forward, knit 3, slip 1, knit 1, draw the slipped over the knitted stitch, knit 1, knit 2 together, knit 3, throw the cotton forward, knit 2 together, throw the cotton forward, knit 2 together, throw the cotton forward, knit 1, throw the cotton forward, knit 1.

26th round: * Knit 1, throw the cotton forward, knit 1, throw the cotton forward 3 times alternately, slip 1, knit 1, draw the first over the last, throw the cotton forward; knit 2, slip 1, knit 1, draw the first over the last, knit 1, knit 2 together, knit 2, three times alternately, throw the cotton forward, knit 2 together, throw the cotton forward, knit 1, throw the cotton forward, knit 1.

28th round: * Knit 1, throw the cotton forward, knit 1, four times alternately, throw the cotton forward, slip 1, knit 1, draw the slipped over the knitted stitch; throw the cotton forward, knit 1, slip 1, knit 1, draw the slipped over the knitted stitch; knit 1, knit 2 together, knit 1, four times alternately throw the cotton forward, knit 2 together, throw the cotton forward, knit 1, throw the cotton forward, knit 1.

30th round: * Knit 1, throw the cotton forward, knit 1, six times alternately throw the cotton forward, slip 1, knit 1, draw the slipped over the knitted stitch, knit 1 six times alternately, knit 2 together, throw the cotton forward, knit 1, throw the cotton forward, knit 1.

32nd round: Knit 1, throw the cotton forward, knit 1, 6 times alternately throw the cotton forward, slip 1, knit 1, draw the slipped over the knitted stitch, throw the cotton forward, knit 3 stitches together, 6 times alternately throw the cotton forward, knit 2 together, throw the cotton forward, knit 1, throw the cotton forward, knit 1.

34th round: * Knit 1, throw the cotton forward, knit 1, 7 times alternately throw the cotton forward, slip 1, knit 1, draw the slipped over the knitted stitch, knit 1, 7 times alternately knit 2 together, throw the cotton forward, knit 1, throw the cotton forward, knit 1.

36th round: * Knit 1, throw the cotton forward, knit 1, 7 times alternately throw the cotton forward, slip 1, knit 1, draw the slipped over the knitted stitch, throw the cotton forward, knit 4 stitches together, 7 times alternately throw the cotton forward, knit 2 together, throw the cotton forward, knit 1, throw the cotton forward, knit 1.

38th round: * Knit 1, throw the cotton forward, knit 1, 8 times alternately throw the cotton forward, slip 1, knit 1, draw the, slipped over the knitted stitch, 8 times alternately knit 2 together, throw the cotton forward, knit 1, throw the cotton forward, knit 1.

40th round: * Knit 1, throw the cotton forward, knit 1, 8 times alternately throw the cotton forward, slip 1, knit 1, draw the slipped over the knitted stitch, throw the cotton forward, knit 3 stitches together as 1 stitch, 8 times alternately throw the cotton forward, knit 2 together, throw the cotton torward, knit 1, throw the cotton forward, knit 1. You now have 41 stitches on each needle; knit 1 round, and cast off.

When completed, the squares are joined together on the wrong side.

Knitted Sleeping Sock

Materials for one pair: 4 ounces white fleecy, 3 ply; 1 ounces light blue fleecy.

These socks are knitted with white and blue wool in a diamond pattern, and in rounds like a stocking. Begin at the upper part of the sock; cast on 103 stitches with blue wool on pretty thick steel knitting-needles, and knit 20 rounds of the diamond pattern as follows:

1st round: Quite plain.

2nd round: Purled; both these rounds are worked with blue wool.

3rd to 6th rounds: Knitted plain with white wool.

7th round: With blue wool; knit 3, draw the wool through the next stitch of the 2nd round worked with blue wool, draw it out as a loop, keep it on the needle, knit again 3 stitches, and so on. 8th round: With blue wool; the loop which has been taken up on the preceding round is purled off together with the preceding stitch. Repeat the 3rd and 8th rounds twice more; the loop of one round must be placed between those of the preceding one. Then knit with white wool 31 rounds, alternately 2 stitches knitted, 2 stitches purled, then work the foot in the diamond pattern in the same way as usual for a stocking. The heel is formed by leaving 23 stitches on each side the seam stitch, and knitted backwards and forwards in the diamond pattern. At the toe decrease so that the decreasings form a seam on both sides of the toe. This is obtained by knitting the 3rd and 4th

235. Knitted Sleeping Sock.

stitches of the 1st needle together; on the 2nd needle slip the 4th stitch before the last, knit the next stitch and draw the slipped stitch over the knitted one; decrease in the same manner on the other 2 needles of this round. Repeat these decreasings exactly in the same direction and at the same places, so that there are always 4 stitches between the 2 decreasings at the end and at the beginning of 2 needles; they always take place after 3 or 2 plain rounds, and at last after 1 plain round. The remaining stitches are knitted off 2 and 2 together. To complete the sock, the outline of the sole is marked by working slip stitches with blue wool in crochet all round it; work also slip stitches on the selvedge stitch of the heel. The stocking is finished off at the top with a double round of loops in blue wool, worked over a mesh four-fifths of an inch wide.

Lady's Knitted Purse

Materials: 2 skeins of black purse silk; 2 skeins of scarlet ditto; black jet beads; a steel clasp with chain; a tassel of black beads; 5 steel knitting-needles.

This purse is knitted with black and scarlet purse silk, and ornamented with black beads and a black bead tassel. Begin the purse with the black silk in the centre of the bottom part, and cast on for one part of it 7 stitches. Knit 14 rows on these backwards and forwards, in such a manner that the work is knitted on one side and purled on the other. The 1st stitch of every row is slipped, the 1st row of this part is purled. * On that side where hangs the thread with which you work take the back chain of the 7 selvedge stitches of the part you have just knitted on a separate needle, and knit another part, which must have 15 rows, and the 1st row of which is knitted. Repeat 10 times more from *. The stitches of several parts can be taken on the same needle, so as not to be hindered in working by too many needles. When the 12th part is completed, take the selvedge stitches on the left hand on another needle, cast them off together with the cast on stitches of the 1st part, and fasten the silk thread. Then take the 7 right-hand selvedge stitches of one black part on a needle, take the red silk on which the beads have been strung and work 15 rows on these stitches, the 1st row from the wrong side, and therefore purled; in the 1st, as well as in all the other purled rows, the last stitch must be purled together with the next stitch of the next black part. In the purled rows, moreover, excepting in the first and last one, a bead must be worked in after casting off the 2nd, 4th, and 6th stitches. The stitch must be worked by inserting the needle into the back part, and in drawing through the silk which has been thrown forward, let the bead slide through the stitch so that it is on the right side of the work. In the following knitted row, the needle must also be inserted into the back part of the bead stitch.

When 12 such red parts have been completed, work again 12 black parts on the selvedge stitch of the same, in which the beads are not knitted in, but sewn on afterwards, when the purse is completed. Then work 3 times more alternately 12 red and 12 black parts; when the last 12 black parts have been completed cast off the stitches of the last black part together with the selvedge stitches, the 1st on the wrong side; the stitches of the 6th part are cast off in the same manner together with the selvedge stitches of the 7th. The red parts which remain to be worked on the black part are thus lessened by 2; the 2nd, 3rd, and 4th, and the 7th, 8th, and 9th of these parts must be by 6 rows longer. Then gather all the stitches and

236. Lady's Knitted Purse.

selvedge stitches of the 10 parts on 2 needles, in such a manner that the 2 black parts, the stitches and selvedge stitches of which have been cast off together, are placed on the sides of the purse, and knit as follows with black silk, first on the stitches of the one needle, and then on those of the other: 1 row knitted, knitting together every 3rd and 4th stitch; then work 3 rows backwards and forwards on the same number of stitches, which must be knitted on the right side; then work 8 rows more in the same manner, casting off the 2 first stitches of the 8 rows. Then cast off all the remaining stitches, sew the beads on the black parts from the illustration; also the clasp and bead tassel.

Knitted Antimacassar or Berceaunelle Cover

Materials: Grey and violet fleecy wool.

This antimacassar, part of which is seen on No. 239, smaller than full size, is made of rosettes and small squares, which are knitted separately with violet and grey fleecy wool with fine knitting-needles. In the middle of each rosette sew on a tatted circle of grey wool. The edge of the antimacassar is ornamented with a grey woollen fringe. For each rosette cast on 6 stitches with violet wool, and knit 12 rows backwards and forwards in such a manner that the work is knitted on one side and purled on the other: the first of these 12 rows is purled, the first stitch of every row is slipped; * then take the first five selvedge stitches of the knitted part on a separate needle (on the side where the end of wool hangs down, leaving it unnoticed for the present), inserting the needle into the back chain of the stitch (the selvedge stitch which is next to the cast-on stitch remains, therefore, unworked upon), and knit on these a new part, which must have 13 rows; the first row is knitted, and in this row work 2 stitches in the first stitch, one purled and one knitted, so that this new part is equally six stitches wide. Repeat 8 times more from *. After having worked several parts, the stitches can, of course, be taken on the same needle, so as not to increase the number of needles. When the 10th

Top left: 237. Square for Antimacassar.

Top right: 238. Rosette for Antimacassar.

Bottom left: 239. Part of Antimacassar.

Bottom right: 240. Knitted Border.

part is completed, take the selvedge stitches of the left-hand side of the same on a separate needle, cast them off with the cast-on stitches of the first part, and fasten the wool. Then take the 6 selvedge stitches on the right hand of one part on a separate needle; take the grey wool, and work on these stitches 13 rows backwards and forwards; the first row is knitted; it is worked on the right side of the work; in this, and in every following knitted row, knit the last stitch together with the next stitch of the next violet part. When 10 such grey parts are completed (each of the remaining 9 parts consists of 13 rows, and begins with one knitted row), take all the stitches and the selvedge stitches of these parts on four needles and knit with these stitches, also with grey wool 1 row knitted, in which the 6 selvedge stitches must be decreased to 3 by knitting always 2 stitches together as 1 stitch; each of the other stitches is knitted as usual. Then purl 2 rows with violet wool, and cast off.

For the tatted circle in the centre of the rosette, work with grey wool a circle consisting of 1 double, and 11 times alternately 1 purl 3-10ths of an inch long, 2 double, then 1 purl and 1 double. The circle is sewn on the rosette, from the illustration, with grey wool. No. 238 shows such a rosette full size. The small squares (see No. 237) are worked with grey wool; cast on 36 stitches, join the stitches into a circle, and purl 2 rows. To form the corners, knit together 4 times 2 stitches after every 7 stitches in the first of these two rounds, in the second round knit together 2 stitches after every 6 stitches; these decreasings and those of the other rounds must always take place, at the same places as in the preceding round. Then take the violet wool, and knit 7 rows; in the first of these knit 4 times 2 stitches together after intervals of 5 stitches; no decreasings take place in the 2nd, 4th, and 6th rows; in the 3rd row knit together 4 times 3 stitches as 1 stitch, and in the 5th and 7th rows 4 times 2 stitches as 1 stitch. After the 7th round, the remaining stitches are cast off together as 1 stitch. Then fasten the wool and cut it off. Lastly, sew the rosettes and squares together from No. 239 for a cover, and edge it round the border with a fringe of grey wool.

Knitted Border

Material: Messrs. Walter Evans and Co.'s No. 10 or No. 50 knitting cotton.

If knitted with thick cotton, this border will be suitable for trimming a quilt or berceaunette cover; if, on the contrary, fine cotton is used, the pattern will form a very pretty collar for a little boy or girl.

To make a collar, begin by a chain of 220 stitches, and work 6 rows backwards and forwards alternately, knitting 4 stitches and purling 2.

In the 2nd, 4th, and 6th rows the 4 stitches are purled, and the 2 are knitted.

7th row: * Purl 2, make 1, knit 2, purl 2. Repeat from *.

8th row: Alternately purl 5, knit 2. All the rows with even numbers are knitted like this, except that the number of the knitted stitches are increased by 2 in each of them. We will not, therefore, henceforth mention these rows.

9th row: * Knit 2, make 1, knit 1, make 1, knit 2, purl 2. Repeat from *.

11th row: * Knit 2, make 1, knit 3, make 1, knit 2, purl 2. Repeat from *.

13th row: * Knit 2, make 1, knit 5, make 1, knit 2, purl 2. Repeat from *. The pattern is continued in the same manner. The small gores formed between the ribs are increased by 2 stitches in every second row. Each of these gores has 13 stitches in the 21st row, which is the last. Cast off all the stitches after this row.

Take a crochet needle, and with the same cotton as that used for the knitting work 1 stitch of double crochet in every stitch of the selvedge, then the 2 following rows for the edging. 1st row: Alternately 1 treble, 1 chain, under which miss 1.

2nd row: Alternately 1 double over 1 treble of preceding row, 1 purl (that is, 5 chain and 1 slip stitch in the first), under which miss 1. Over the first row of the knitting work 1 row of close double crochet. The border is now completed.

Knee-Cap in Knitting

Materials: For 1 pair, 4 oz. pink 4-thread fleecy wool, and a small quantity of white ditto.

Begin each knee-cap by casting on with pink wool 114 stitches, equally divided upon 4 needles, and joining them into a circle. Upon this number of stitches work 47 rounds, alternately knitting and purling 2 stitches. In the 48th round begin the gore which covers the knee; it is worked separately backward and forwards, always alternately knitting and purling 2 stitches.

After 2 rows change the pattern, so as to form small squares Knit the first row of this gore upon 26 stitches slipped off from the last row on to a separate needle. At the end of each following row knit the nearest stitch of the nearest needle, so as to increase 1 stitch in each row of the gore.

Continue in this way until only 42 stitches remain of the ribbed part. After this work the remainder of the gore separately, decreasing once at the beginning and end of each row till only 26 stitches remain; then take up 23 stitches of the selvedge on each side of these 26 stitches, and work 47 rounds, alternately knitting and purling 2 stitches.

The edging at the top and bottom of the knee-cap is worked in crochet. With white wool make a chain of 50 stitches; turn and work 1 row of crochet *à tricoter*; then work a second row thus: the first part, as usual, with white, but coming back, with pink make 4 chain between each stitch, work in the same way on the other side of the foundation chain, thus forming a small ruche, and sew it on to the edge of the knitting.

241. Knee-Cap in Knitting.

Knitted Neckerchief in Black Shetland Wool

Material: Black Shetland wool.

This three-cornered neckerchief is knitted in the following pattern (commencing at the corner). 1st row: slip 1, make 1, knit 2 together, inserting the needle into the back part of the stitch, slip 1, make 1, knit 2 together. 2nd row: Knit 1, purl 1 in the stitch formed by throwing the wool forward in the preceding row; the other stitches are purled. In the next row the holes are alternated; the neckerchief must of course be increased at the beginning and end of every other row. It measures at the upper edge 1 yard 16 inches across from one corner to the other; the lower

242. Knitted Neckerchief in Shetland Wool.

corner is rounded off. The neckerchief is edged with a knitted lace.

The lace is worked in rows backwards and forwards, the cross way. Cast on 22 stitches and work the 1st row as follows: Slip 1, knit 11, knit 2 together, throw the wool forward, knit 2 together, knit 6.

2nd row: Slip 1, purl 18, knit 1 and purl 1 with the stitch formed in the preceding row by throwing the wool forward.

3rd row; Slip 1, knit 2 together, knit 9, knit 2 together, throw the wool forward, knit 2 together, throw the wool forward, knit 2 together, knit 5.

4th row: Slip 1, purl 5, knit 1, purl 1, knit 1 in the stitch formed in the preceding row by throwing the wool forward, purl 13.

5th row: Slip 1, knit 2 together, knit 6, knit 2 together, throw the wool forward, knit 2 together, throw the wool forward, knit 2 together, throw the wool forward, knit 2 together, knit 4.

6th row: Slip 1, purl 8, knit 1, purl 1 in the stitch formed by throwing the wool forward in preceding row, purl 9.

7th row: Slip 1, knit 2 together, knit 4, knit 2 together, throw the wool forward 4 times alternately, knit 2 together, knit 4.

8th row: Slip 1, purl 3, knit 1, purl 1 in the stitch formed by throwing the wool forward in the preceding row, purl 13.

9th row: Slip 1, knit 2 together, knit 2, 5 times alternately; knit 2 together, throw the wool forward, knit 2 together, knit 2.

10th row: Slip 1, knit 1, purl 1 in the stitch formed by throwing the wool forward in preceding row, purl 5.

11th row: Slip 1, knit 2 together, 6 times alternately knit 2 together, throw the wool forward, knit 2 together, knit 1.

12th row: Slip 1, knit 1 in the stitch formed by throwing the wool forward in preceding row, purl 13.

13th row: Slip 1, throw the wool forward, knit 2, knit 2 together, 5 times alternately throw the wool forward, knit 2 together, knit 2.

14th row: Slip 1, purl 10, knit 1, purl 1 in the stitch formed by throwing the wool forward in preceding row, purl 5.

15th row: Slip 1, throw the wool forward, knit 4, knit 2 together, 4 times alternately throw the wool forward, knit 2 together, knit 3.

16th row: Slip 1, purl 3, knit 1, purl 1 in the stitch formed by throwing the wool forward in preceding row, purl 13.

17th row: Slip 1, throw the wool forward, knit 6, knit 2 together, 3 times alternately throw the wool forward, knit 2 together, knit 4.

18th row: Slip 1, purl 8, knit 1, purl 1 in the stitch formed by throwing the wool forward in preceding row, purl 9.

19th row: Slip 1, throw the wool forward, knit 8, knit 2 together, twice alternately throw the wool forward, knit 2 together, knit 5.

20th row: Slip 1, purl 5, knit 1, purl 1 in the stitch formed by throwing the wool forward in preceding row, purl 13.

21st row: Slip 1, throw the wool forward, knit 10, knit 2 together, throw the wool forward, knit 2 together, knit 6.

22nd row: Slip 1, purl 6, knit 1, purl 1 in the stitch formed by throwing the wool forward in preceding row.

23rd row: Slip 1, throw the wool forward, knit 12, knit 2 together, knit 7.

24th row: Purled. Repeat from the 1st row till the lace is sufficiently long. Then sew on the lace round the edge; the lace can be knitted somewhat narrower for the upper edge. One of the ends of the neckerchief is knotted, As seen in the illustration, and the other end is drawn through the knot.

Knitted Bodice Without Sleeves

Materials: 4 ounces black, 3-½ ounces purple fleecy; black silk elastic; a steel buckle; 9 black bone buttons.

This bodice is knitted in brioche stitch with black and purple wool, so that the raised ribs appear black on one side and purple on the other. The bodice fits quite close. It is fastened in front with black bone buttons and a steel buckle. Two strips of silk elastic are knitted in at the bottom. Begin at the bottom of the bodice with black wool, and cast on 170 stitches. The needles must be rather fine, and the knitting not too loose. Work backwards and forwards 24 rows as follows:

Slip the 1st stitch, alternately throw the wool forward, slip 1 as if you were going to purl it, and knit 1. In the next row knit together the stitch which has been slipped and the stitch formed by throwing the wool forward, slip the knitted stitch, after having thrown the wool forward. In the 25th row take the purple wool and work 1 row as before. Now work alternately 1 row with black wool and 1 row with purple, but as the wool is not cut off, the brioche stitch must be alternately knitted and purled. Work always 2 rows on the same side from right to left. The following 26th row is worked with black wool in common brioche stitch, only the slipped stitch of the preceding row is purled together with the stitch formed by throwing the wool forward.

27th row: Turn the work, with purple wool purled brioche stitch.

28th row: On the same side with black wool knitted brioche stitch. After having worked 40 rows all in the same

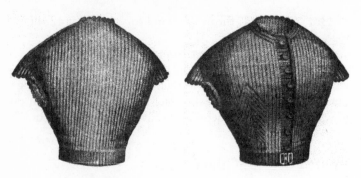

Left: 243. Knitted Bodice without Sleeves (Back).

Right: 244. Knitted Bodice without Sleeves (Front).

manner, begin the front gore. Divide the stitches upon three needles, 82 stitches on one needle for the back, and 44 stitches for each front part on the two other needles. Then work the first 11 stitches of the left front part (this row must be worked on that side of the work upon which the ribs appear purple) in knitted brioche stitch; the 11th stitch must have a slipped stitch, with the wool thrown forward, therefore it is a purple rib. After this stitch begin the gore with the following 13 stitches. The ribs are then worked so that a purple one comes over a black one, and a black one over a purple one. Do not work upon the following black stitch; knit the following stitch with the one formed by throwing the wool forward. Throw the wool forward, and then only slip the black stitch which had been left, so that it comes behind the stitch which has just been knitted. This crossing of the stitch is repeated once more, then knit the following stitch together with the one formed by throwing the wool forward, throw the wool forward, slip the crossed black stitch and the two following single black stitches. The slipped stitch and the stitch formed by throwing the wool forward before the 3rd single black stitch are then knitted together, so that the crossed stitches are placed in opposite directions. The three black stitches which are knitted off together as 1 stitch in the next row form the middle line of the front gore, and are continued in a straight line to the point of the gore. The crossing takes place twice in this row, but now the black stitch is slipped first. After the 24th stitch knit together the following stitch with the stitch formed by throwing the wool forward. Then continue to work in common brioche stitch to the other front part, where the gore begins before the 24th stitch from the end. In the next row, which is worked in purled brioche stitch with black wool, take up the black loop between two purple ribs after the 11th stitch; purl it so as to form the stitch which is missing at that place. The 3 slipped stitches in the preceding row are purled together as one stitch with the stitch formed by throwing the wool forward between the ribs. The loop is also taken up on the other side of the front gore in the same manner, as well as on the other front part. Then work 6 rows without increasing or decreasing. The crossing of the stitch is repeated after every 7 rows, always on the knitted brioche stitch side, with purple wool. In the 18th row of the gore the 3 middle stitches are not knitted together, but separately, so that the pattern must be decreased in 26 rows. In the back 30 stitches only must be decreased, two in every 6th row.

After the 60th row another decreasing takes place on the outer edges of the front parts for the neck; they decrease 2 stitches (1st rib) after the 5th stitch from the front edge in every 3rd row. The 5 stitches which close to the neck are cast off together with the 5 stitches on the shoulders. Then cast off loosely the stitches of the back; take all the selvedge stitches of the front on the needles, and knit 24 rows of brioche stitch with black wool, making 9 button-holes on the right front part. On the wrong side of this part sew on a strip of black silk, with slits worked round in button-hole stitch, stitching at the same time into the knitting. The following scallops are knitted round the top of the jacket and round the armholes with black wool: Take the selvedge stitches on the needles, work 4 rows alternately, 1 stitch knitted, 1 stitch purled, thread the wool into a Berlin wool-work needle, * cast off 3 stitches together, draw the wool through the needle, and take the 2 following stitches on the wool in the worsted-needle; repeat from *. Sew on the buttons the strips of silk elastic on either side of the black stripe at the bottom, and fasten the ends of the latter with the steel buckle.

Baby's Boot

Materials for one pair: ½ ounce red, ½ ounce white, Berlin wool; steel knitting-needles.

This pretty boot consists of a shoe knitted in red wool, and a sock in white wool ornamented with red. Begin the knitting with the upper scalloped edge of the latter. Cast on 96 stitches with red wool, divide them on four needles, and knit in rounds as follows: 1st and 2nd rounds: With red wool, purled.

3rd to 8th round: With white wool.

3rd round: Knitted.

4th round: * Knit 4, throw the wool forward, knit 1, throw the wool forward, knit 4, knit 3 together. Repeat 7 times more from *.

5th round: Knitted; the stitches formed by throwing the wool forward are knitted as one stitch. Knit 3 stitches together at the place where 3 stitches were knitted together in the 4th round, so that the decreasing of the preceding round forms the middle stitch of the 3 stitches to be decreased in this round.

6th and 7th rounds: Like the 5th.

8th round: Knitted; you must have 48 stitches left.

9th to 11th round: With red wool. 9th round: Knitted.

10th and 11th rounds: Purled.

12th to 30th round: With white wool.

12th round: Knitted.

13th round to 30th round: Alternately purl 1, knit 1, inserting the needle in the back part of the stitch.

245. Baby's Boot.

31st to 33rd round: With red wool.

31st round: Knitted.

32nd round and 33rd round: Purled.

34th and 35th rounds: With white wool. 34th round: Knitted.

35th round: Alternately throw the wool forward, knit 2 together. Each stitch formed by throwing the wool forward is knitted as one stitch in the next round.

36th to 38th round: With red wool.

36th round: Knitted.

37th and 38th rounds: Purled.

39th to 47th round: With white wool. Alternately purl 1, slip 1, as if you were going to purl it; the wool must lie in front of the slipped stitch; in the following rounds take care to purl the slipped stitches.

Take now 18 stitches for the front gored sock part (leave 30 stitches untouched), and work backwards and forwards with red wool. 48th to 50th row: With red wool.

48th row: Knitted.

49th row: Purled.

50th row: Knitted.

51st to 85th row: With white wool in the pattern described in the 39th round. But as you work backwards and forwards you must alternately knit and purl the stitches. Decrease 1 stitch at the beginning and at the end of the 84th and 85th rows; decrease 1 stitch in the middle of the 85th row, so that the 85th row has 13 stitches left. After this work with red wool.

86th row: Knitted.

87th row: Knit 1, purl 2, knit 1, purl 2, knit 1, purl 2, knit 1, purl 2, knit 1.

Repeat these last 2 rows 3 times more and knit plain to the 94th, decreasing one, however, on each side. Now work with the whole number of stitches, taking up the selvedge stitches of the gored part and dividing them with the 30 other stitches on four needles. Knit once more in rounds; the next 20 rounds are alternately 1 round knitted, 1 round purled. In the 2 last knitted rounds decrease twice close together in the middle of the back part of the shoe. Knit 8 rounds; in every other round decrease twice in the middle of the front of the shoe, leaving 9 stitches between the two decreasings. The number of stitches between the decreasings decreases with every round, so that the decreasings form slanting lines meeting in a point. Cast off after these 8 rounds, by knitting together 2 opposite stitches on the wrong side. The sock part is edged with a raised red border, which is worked by taking all the red stitches of the 1st round of the shoe on the needle and knitting 4 rounds, so as to leave the purled side of the stitch always outside; then cast off very tight. Draw a piece of braid through the open-work row in the sock part, and finish it off at either end with tassels to match.

Knitted Border for a Bedquilt

Materials: Messrs. Walter Evans and Co.'s No. 8 white knitting cotton; thick steel pins.

Cast on a sufficient number of stitches for the length of the border, which must be able to be divided by 31; knit 4 plain rows:

5th row: Alternately make 1, knit 2 together.

Then 5 more plain rows.

Now begin the pattern: 1st row: * Make 1, knit 1 slantways

246. Knitted Border for a Bedquilt.

(to knit a stitch slantways, insert the needle from the front to the back and from right to left); † purl 5; knit 1 slantways. Repeat from † 4 times more than from * to the end of the row.

2nd row: Purled.

3rd row: Knit 2, * make 1; knit 1 slantways; † purl 5; knit 1 slantways. Repeat from † four times more. Repeat from * to the end of the row.

4th row: The same as the second.

The continuation of the work is clearly shown in our illustration. The increasing caused by knitting the made stitches is regularly repeated in each second row, so that the stitches between the striped divisions increase, and form large triangles; the striped divisions, on the other hand, are narrowed so as to form the point of the triangles. To obtain this result, decrease five times in the 6th, 12th, 18th, and 24th rows, by purling together the two last stitches of one purled division, so that each division has but eleven stitches left in the 25th row. In the 28th row knit together one purled stitch with one knitted slantways, so that there will be only 6 stitches left for each division; these stitches are knitted slantways in the 29th and 30th rows. In the 31st row they are knitted together, two and two. There remain in each division three more stitches, which are knitted together in the 34th row. Two rows entirely purled complete the upper edge of the border.

Knitted Quilt

Materials: 8-thread fleecy wool; wooden needles.

This pattern may be worked in narrow strips of different colours, and in that case each strip should contain 1 row of patterns; or the quilt may be composed of wide strips with several rows of patterns, those of one row being placed between those of the preceding. In the first case, that is if you work narrow strips, you may use several colours; but if wide strips are preferred, they should be of two colours only. Our pattern was worked in wide strips, alternately grey and red. Each strip is knitted the short way.

For a strip with five raised patterns in the width cast on 20 stitches.

2nd row: Right side of the work. Slip 1, purl 1, * make 1, purl 4. Repeat from * 3 times more; make 1, purl 2.

3rd row: Slip 1, knit all the stitches that were purled in the preceding row, and purl all those that were made.

247. Knitted Quilt.

4th row: Slip 1, purl 1, * knit 1, make 1, purl 4. Repeat from * 3 times more; knit 1, make 1, purl 2.

5th row: Slip 1, knit all the purled stitches, purl all the rest.

6th row: Slip 1, purl 1, * knit 2, make 1, purl 4. Repeat from * 3 times more; knit 2, make 1, purl 2.

7th row: The same as the 5th.

8th row: Slip 1, purl 1, * knit 3, make 1, purl 4, and so on.

9th row: The same as the 5th row.

10th row: Slip 1, purl 1, * slip 1, knit 1, pass the slipped stitch over the knitted one, knit 2, purl 4, repeat from *.

11th row: Knit all the purled stitches, purl all the rest.

12th row: Slip 1, purl 1, * slip 1, knit 1, pass the slipped stitch over, knit 1, purl 4, and repeat from *.

13th row: The same as the 11th.

14th row: Slip 1, purl 1, * slip 1, knit 1, pass the slipped stitch over, purl 4, and repeat.

15th row: Slip 1, * knit 2 together, knit 3. Repeat from * 3 times more; knit 2 together, knit 2.

The second row of patterns begins with the 16th row. There are only 4 in this 2nd row, so that after the 1st slipped stitch you purl 3 stitches instead of 1, and in the 2nd row, after the 4th made stitch, you purl 4 more stitches. Repeat alternately these 2 rows of raised patterns, and when you have a sufficient number of strips sew them together. Trim the quilt all round with a knotted fringe.

Stitch in Knitting, for Couvrettes, Comforters, Opera Caps, Carriage Shawls, Jackets, &c.

Materials: Messrs. Walter Evans and Co.'s knitting cotton No. 20, or fine wool.

Cast on an uneven number of stitches.

1st row: Slip 1, * make 1, knit 1, make 1, knit 1. Repeat from *.

2nd row: Slip 1, * knit 2 together, and repeat from * to the end of the row.

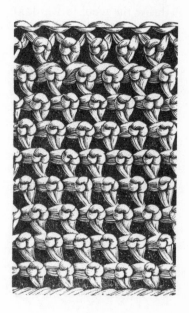

248. Stitch for Couvrettes, Comforters, &c.

Knitted Veil

Material: Fine Shetland wool.

Illustration 249 represents a knitted veil in reduced size. The original was worked with fine Shetland wool in an open pattern; it is edged with a knitted lace. Its length is 24 inches, its width 18 inches. Work the veil from a paper pattern of a shape corresponding to that of illustration 249. Compare the paper shape often with the knitting in the course of the work, and try to keep them alike.

Knit the veil in the pattern of the original, or in the pattern of illustration 250. For the former one begin at the lower edge of the veil, cast on 45 stitches upon thick wooden needles, and work the 1st row: * Knit 2, throw the wool forward, knit 2 together twice, repeat from *.

2nd row: Purled.

3rd row: Knit 1, throw the wool forward, knit 2 together, * throw the wool forward, knit 2 together twice, and repeat from *.

4th row: Purled.

5th row: Like the 2nd row. The pattern must be reversed. The pattern figures increase with the increasings at the beginning and at the end of each row.

The pattern of illustration 250 consists of the 2 following

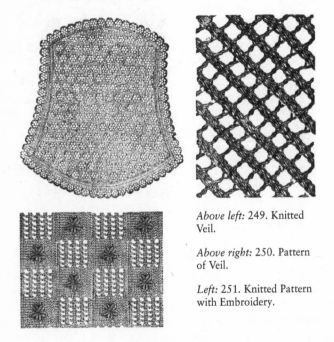

Above left: 249. Knitted Veil.

Above right: 250. Pattern of Veil.

Left: 251. Knitted Pattern with Embroidery.

rows: 1st row: Slip 1, then alternately throw the wool forward, and knit 2 together.

2nd row: Entirely knitted; make 1 stitch of the wool thrown forward in the last row. When the veil is finished, wet it, and stretch it over paper or pasteboard; let it dry, and then edge it with the following lace: Cast on 10, knit the 1st.

2nd row: Knit 1, throw the wool forward, knit 9.

3rd row: Knitted.

4th row: Knit 1, throw the wool forward, knit 2, throw the wool forward, knit 2 together twice, knit 4.

5th row: Knitted.

6th row: Knit 1, throw the wool forward, knit 2, throw the wool forward, knit 2 together 3 times, knit 3.

7th row: Cast off 3 stitches, knit 10. 8th row: Knitted.

Knitted Pattern with Raised Embroidery

Materials: Messrs. Walter Evans and Co.'s knitting cotton No. 8 or 20.

This pattern is worked in rows going backwards and forwards with thick or fine cotton according to the use you wish to make of it. The star-like figures on the knitted squares are worked with soft cotton in *point de poste*. Cast on a number of stitches long enough (19 stitches are necessary for the two squares), work the 1st row: * Knit 11 stitches, alternately 4 times knit 2 together, throw the cotton forward. Repeat from *.

The 2nd row is worked like the 1st, only purled; in this row, as well as in the following ones, the stitch must be knitted with the cotton thrown forward after the stitch; the last stitch of a plain square with the first cotton thrown forward of the open-work figure. The number of stitches in the last must always be 8. The pattern consists alternately of these two rows. Each pattern contains 12 rows, with the 13th the squares are reversed. The star figures are embroidered with double cotton by working 5 chain stitch in the middle of each square; draw the needle underneath the knitting to the next centre of a square.

Knitted Table Cover

Materials: Messrs. Walter Evans and Co.'s coarse knitting cotton; thick steel knitting-needles.

This cover is suitable for either a large or a small table, as the pattern may be increased as much as required. It is suitable for antimacassars. Cast on 4 stitches, join them into a circle, and work the 1st round four times alternately. Throw the cotton forward, knit 1.

2nd round: Entirely knitted.

3rd round: * Throw the cotton forward, knit 1. Repeat 7 times more from *. After every pattern round knit 1 round plain. Until after the 21st round, we shall not mention this any more.

5th round: * Throw the cotton forward, knit 2 *. From the 7th to the 12th round the knitted stitches in every other round increase by 1 stitch, so that in the 12th round there

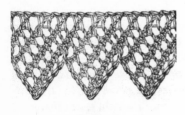

252. Table-Cover Border.

253. Knitted Table Cover.

are 7 stitches between those formed by throwing the cotton forward.

13th round: * Throw the cotton forward, knit 2 together, knit 4, knit 2 together *.

15th round: * Throw the cotton forward, knit 1, throw the cotton forward, knit 2 together, knit 2, knit 2 together *.

17th round: * Throw the cotton forward, knit 3, throw the cotton forward, knit 2 together, knit 2 together *.

19th round: * Throw the cotton forward, knit 5, throw the cotton forward, knit 2 together, *.

21st round: * Knit 1, throw the cotton forward, knit 5, throw the cotton forward, knit 2 *.

22nd round: * Knit 2, knit 2 together, knit 1, knit 2 together, knit 3 *.

23rd round: * Knit 2, throw the cotton forward, knit 3, throw the cotton forward, knit 3 *.

24th round: * Knit 3, knit 2 together, knit 5 *.

25th round: * Knit 3, throw the cotton forward, knit 2 together, throw the cotton forward, knit 4.

26th round: Entirely knitted *.

27th round: * Throw the cotton forward, knit 9, throw the cotton forward, knit 1 *.

28th round: Entirely knitted.

29th round: * Knit 1, throw the cotton forward, knit 9, throw the cotton forward, knit 2 *.

30th round: Entirely knitted.

31st round: * Knit 2, throw the cotton forward, knit 9, throw the cotton forward, knit 3 *.

32nd round: Entirely knitted.

33rd round: * Knit 3, throw the cotton forward, knit 9, throw the cotton forward, knit 4 *.

34th round: * Knit 4, knit 2 together, knit 5, knit 2 together, knit 5 *.

35th round: * Knit 4, throw the cotton forward, knit 7, throw the cotton forward, knit 5 *.

36th round: * Knit 5, knit 2 together, knit 3, knit 2 together, knit 6 *.

37th round: * Throw the cotton forward, knit 5 three times, throw the cotton forward, knit 1 *.

38th round: * Knit 7, knit 2 together, knit 1, knit 2 together, knit 8 *.

39th round: * Knit 1, throw the cotton forward, knit 6, throw the cotton forward, knit 3. throw the cotton forward, knit 6, throw the cotton forward, knit 2 *.

40th round: * Knit 9, knit 3 together, knit 10*.

41st round: * Knit 2, throw the cotton forward, knit 15, throw the cotton forward, knit 3 *.

42nd round: * Knit 3, knit 2 together, knit 11, knit 2 together, knit 4 *.

43rd round: * Knit 3, throw the cotton forward, knit 13, throw the cotton forward, knit 4 *.

44th round: * Knit 4, knit 2 together, knit 9, knit 2 together, knit 5 *.

When the cover is completed, edge it all round, with the following border worked the short way: Cast on 5 stitches and knit the 1st row, slip 1, throw the cotton forward, knit 2 together, throw the cotton forward, knit 2.

2nd row: Slip 1, knit the rest. Repeat this row after every pattern row.

3rd row: Slip 1, throw the cotton forward, knit 2 together, throw the cotton forward, knit 2 together, throw the cotton forward, knit 1.

5th row: Slip 1, throw the cotton forward, knit 2 together, throw the cotton forward, knit 2 together, throw the cotton forward, knit 2.

7th row: Slip 1, throw the cotton forward, knit 2 together, throw the cotton forward, knit 2 together, throw the cotton forward, knit 2 together, throw the cotton forward, knit 1.

9th row: Slip 1, throw the cotton forward, knit 2 together, throw the cotton forward, knit 2 together, throw the cotton forward, knit 2 together, throw the cotton forward, knit 2.

11th row: Slip 1, throw the cotton forward, knit 2 together, throw the cotton forward, knit 2 together, throw the cotton forward, knit 2 together, throw the cotton forward, knit 2 together, knit 1.

13th row: Slip 1, throw the cotton forward, knit 2 together, throw the cotton forward, knit 2 together, throw the cotton forward, knit 2 together, throw the cotton forward, knit 2 together, throw the cotton forward, knit 2.

15th round: Cast off 8 stitches, throw the cotton forward, knit 2 together, throw the cotton forward, knit 1.

16th round: Entirely knitted. Begin again at the 1st row, knit a sufficient length of the border, and then trim the cover with it on the outer edge.

Looped Knitting

Materials: 4-thread fleecy wool; 2 wooden knitting-needles; 1 flat wooden mesh.

Cast on a sufficient number of stitches, and knit the 1st row plain.

2nd Row. – Slip the 1st stitch; insert the needle into the next stitch, and throw the cotton forward as if you were going to knit the stitch; place the mesh behind the needle in the right hand, and turn the wool which is on this needle upwards, bring it back again on the needle so that it is wound once round the mesh, and twice round the needle. Then only the double stitch through the second stitch, knit it, and insert the needle into the next stitch, and repeat what has been explained. Knit the last stitch without a loop.

3rd Row. – Before drawing out the mesh, turn the work and knit one plain row. Every double stitch is knitted as one stitch, so as to attain the same number of stitches as in the 1st row.

4th Row. – Like the 2nd row. Repeat these rows as often as required.

This knitting is chiefly used for borders of mats.

254. Looped Knitting.

Knitted Pattern for Comforters

Materials: 4-thread fleecy; 2 wooden knitting-needles.

Cast on a sufficient number of stitches.

1st row: * 3 stitches in the first stitch, knit 1, purl 1, knit 1, knit 3 stitches together, repeat from *.

2nd row: Plain knitting.

3rd row: Purled.

4th row: Knitted. Repeat these four rows, only in the next row the 3 stitches knitted together are worked on the 3 stitches worked in 1 stitch, and the 3 stitches to be worked in 1 stitch are to be placed on the one formed by knitting 3 stitches together.

255. Pattern for Comforters.

Knitted D'Oyley

Materials: Messrs. Walter Evans and Co.'s crochet cotton No. 36; glazed embroidery cotton No. 10; steel knitting-needles.

This pattern is knitted with very fine crochet cotton. The middle part as well as the lace border are worked separately; the latter is sewn on to the middle part. The spots in the thick parts are worked in afterwards with coarser cotton. Commence the pattern in the centre, cast on 6 stitches, join them into a circle, and knit 2 plain rounds.

3rd round: Alternately knit 1, throw the cotton forward.

4th and 5th rounds: Plain.

6th round: Alternately knit 1, throw the cotton forward.

7th round: Plain. Every other round is plain. We shall not mention these plain rounds any more.

8th round: Knit 2, * throw the cotton forward, knit 1, throw the cotton forward, knit 3; repeat from * to the end of the round; lastly, throw the cotton forward, knit 1, throw the cotton forward, knit 1.

10th round: * Throw the cotton forward, knit 1, throw the cotton forward, knit 2 together.

12th round: * Throw the cotton forward, knit 3, throw the cotton forward, knit 2 together, throw the cotton forward, knit 1, throw the cotton forward, knit 2 together.

14th round: * Throw the cotton forward, knit 5, throw the cotton forward,

256. Knitted D'Oyley.

knit 2 together, throw the cotton forward, knit 1, throw the cotton forward, knit 2 together.

16th round: * Throw the cotton forward, knit 7, throw the cotton forward, knit 2 together, throw the cotton forward, knit 1, throw the cotton forward, knit 2 together. The

18th, 20th, 22nd, and 24th rounds are worked like the 16th round; only the middle plain part of the pattern figures increases by 2 stitches in every pattern round, so that there are 15 plain stitches in the 24th round between the 2 stitches formed on either side of the same by throwing the cotton forward.

26th round: * Throw the cotton forward, knit 6, knit 2 together, throw the cotton forward, knit 1, throw the cotton forward, knit 2 together, knit 6, throw the cotton forward, knit 2 together, knit 1, knit 2 together.

28th round: * Throw the cotton forward, knit 6, knit 2 together, throw the cotton forward, knit 3, throw the cotton forward, knit 2 together, knit 6, throw the cotton forward, knit 2 together, knit 1.

30th round: * Knit 1, throw the cotton forward, knit 2 together, knit 6, throw the cotton forward knit 3 together, throw the cotton forward, knit 6, knit 2 together, throw the cotton forward, knit 1, throw the cotton forward, knit 2 together, throw the cotton forward.

32nd round: * Knit 2 together, throw the cotton forward, knit 2 together, knit 13, knit 2 together, throw the cotton forward, knit 2 together, throw the cotton forward, knit 3, throw the cotton forward.

34th round: * Knit 2 together, throw the cotton forward, knit 2 together, knit 11, knit 2 together, throw the cotton forward, knit 2 together, throw the cotton forward, knit 5, throw the cotton forward.

36th round: * Knit 2 together, throw the cotton forward, knit 2 together, knit 9, knit 2 together, throw the cotton forward, knit 2 together, throw the cotton forward, knit 1, throw the cotton forward, knit 2 together, knit 1, knit 2 together, throw the cotton forward, knit 1, throw the cotton forward.

38th round: * Knit 2 together, throw the cotton forward, knit 2 together, knit 7, knit 2 together, throw the cotton forward, knit 2 together, throw the cotton forward, knit 3, throw the cotton forward, knit 3 together, throw the cotton forward, knit 3, throw the cotton forward.

40th round: * Knit 2 together, throw the cotton forward, knit 2 together, knit 5, knit 2 together, throw the cotton forward, knit 2 together, throw the cotton forward, knit 1, throw the cotton forward, knit 2, knit 2 together, throw the cotton forward, knit 1, throw the cotton forward, knit 2 together, knit 2, throw the cotton forward, knit 1, throw the cotton forward.

42nd round: * Knit 2 together, throw the cotton forward, knit 2 together, knit 3, knit 2 together, throw the cotton forward, knit 2 together, throw the cotton forward, knit 3, throw the cotton forward, knit 3 together, throw the cotton forward, knit 3, throw the cotton forward, knit 3 together, throw the cotton forward, knit 3, throw the cotton forward.

44th round: * Knit 2 together, throw the cotton forward, knit 2 together, knit 1, knit 2 together, throw the cotton forward, knit 2 together, throw the cotton forward, knit 3, knit 2 together, throw the cotton forward, knit 1, throw the cotton forward, knit 2 together, knit 3, throw the cotton forward, knit 1, throw the cotton forward, knit 5, throw the cotton forward.

45th and 46th rounds: Plain, then cast off loosely.

For the lace border, which is worked in the short way

backwards and forwards, cast on 22 stitches and knit as follows: 1st row: Slip 1, knit 1, throw the cotton forward, knit 2 together, throw the cotton forward, knit 2 together, throw the cotton forward, knit 2 together, knit 4, knit 2 together, throw the cotton forward, knit 2, knit 2 together, throw the cotton forward, knit 1, throw the cotton forward, knit 2 together.

2nd row: Slip 1, throw the cotton forward, knit 3, throw the cotton forward, knit 2 together, knit 2, throw the cotton forward, knit 2 together, knit 11.

3rd row: Slip 1, knit 9, knit 2 together, throw the cotton forward, knit 2, knit 2 together, throw the cotton forward, knit 5, throw the cotton forward, knit 1.

4th row: Slip 1, throw the cotton forward, knit 7, throw the cotton forward, knit 2 together, knit 2, throw the cotton forward, knit 2 together, knit 9.

5th row: Slip 1, knit 1, throw the cotton forward, knit 2 together, throw the cotton forward, knit 2 together, throw the cotton forward, knit 2 together, knit 2 together, throw the cotton forward, knit 2, knit 2 together, throw the cotton forward, knit 9, throw the cotton forward, knit 1.

6th row: Knit 2 together (knit together the stitch and the next stitch formed by throwing the cotton forward), throw the cotton forward, knit 2 together, knit 5, knit 2 together, throw the cotton forward, knit 2, knit 2 together, throw the cotton forward, knit 10.

7th row: Slip 1, knit 10, throw the cotton forward, knit 2 together, knit 2, throw the cotton forward, knit 2 together, knit 3, knit 2 together, throw the cotton forward, knit 2 together (stitch formed by throwing the cotton forward and the next stitch).

8th row: Knit 2 together, throw the cotton forward, knit 2 together, knit 1, knit 2 together, throw the cotton forward, knit 2, knit 2 together, throw the cotton forward, knit 12.

9th row: Slip 1, knit 1, throw the cotton forward, knit 2 together, throw the cotton forward, knit 2 together, throw the cotton forward, knit 2 together, knit 5, throw the cotton forward, knit 2 together, knit 2, throw the cotton forward, knit 3 together, throw the cotton forward, knit 2 together.

10th row: Knit 2 together, throw the cotton forward, knit 1, throw the cotton forward, knit 2, knit 2 together, throw the cotton forward, knit 14.

11th row: Slip 1, knit 11, knit 2 together, throw the cotton forward, knit 2, knit 2 together, throw the cotton forward, knit 1, throw the cotton forward, knit 3 together. Then begin again on the 2nd row, and work on till the border is long enough; sew the lace on to the centre, slightly gathering the former. Lastly, work in the spots with glazed or coarse embroidery cotton.

Knitted Braces

Material: Messrs. Walter Evans and Co.'s knitting cotton No. 8 or 12.

These braces are knitted with coarse white cotton, taken double; the braces themselves are worked in brioche stitch, the lappets are knitted plain. Begin at the bottom of the front lappet, make a foundation chain of 14 stitches, knit 5 rows plain backwards and forwards, then divide the stitches into two halves to form the button-hole; knit 15 rows on each of the halves consisting of 7 stitches; then take the 14 stitches again on one needle and work 17 rows on them. Then work a second button-hole like the first one; knit 6 more rows plain, increasing 1 at the end of every row, so that the number of stitches at the end of the lappet is 20.

Then begin the pattern in brioche stitch; it is worked as follows: Knit first 1 row, then slip the first stitch of the first following pattern row, *

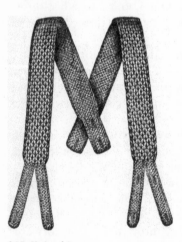

257. Knitted Braces.

throw the cotton forward, slip the next stitch (slip the stitches always as if you were going to purl them), knit 2 together; repeat 5 times more from *; the last stitch is knitted.

2nd row of the pattern: Slip the 1st stitch, * knit 2; the stitch which has been formed in the preceding row by throwing the cotton forward is slipped after the 2nd knitted stitch; repeat 5 times more from *; knit the last stitch.

3rd row: Slip the 1st stitch, * decrease 1 (here, and in all the following rows, knit the next stitch together with the stitch before it, which has been formed in the preceding row by throwing the cotton forward), throw the cotton forward, slip 1; repeat from *; knit the last stitch.

4th row: Slip the 1st stitch, * knit 1, slip the stitch which has been formed in the preceding row by throwing the cotton forward, knit 1, knit the last stitch. Repeat these 4 rows till the braces are long enough. The pattern is 19 inches long. Then knit 6 rows plain, decreasing 1 at the end of every row, then work each lappet separately, dividing the stitches so that each lappet is 7 stitches wide. Each lappet has 72 rows; after the first 18 rows make a button-hole as described for the preceding one. Work 18 rows between the 1st and 2nd button-hole. The lappets are rounded off by decreasing after the 2nd button-hole.

Pattern for Knitted Curtains, &c.

Material: Messrs. Walter Evans and Co.'s knitting cotton No. 8.

This pattern is suitable for knitting different articles, according to the thickness of the cotton used. The number of stitches must be divided by ten. The pattern is knitted backwards and forwards.

1st row: All plain.

2nd row: * Knit 1, make 2, slip 1, knit 1, pass the slipped stitch over the knitted one, knit 5, knit 2 together, make 2. Repeat from *.

3rd row: Purl the long stitch formed by making 2 in preceding row, * make 2, purl 2 together, purl 3, purl 2 together, make 2, purl 3. Repeat from *. (By make 2 is meant twist the cotton twice round the needle, which forms one long stitch, and is knitted or purled as such in next row.)

4th row: Knit 3, * make 2, slip 1, knit 1, and pass the slipped stitch over, knit 1, knit 2 together, make 2, knit 5. Repeat from *.

5th row: Purl 3, * make 2, purl 3 together, make 2, purl 7. Repeat from*.

6th row: Knit 3, * knit 2 together (1 stitch and 1 long stitch), make 2, knit 1, make 2, slip 1, knit 1, pass the slipped stitch over (the knitted stitch is a long stitch), knit 5. Repeat from *.

Continue the pattern by repeating always from the 2nd to

the 5th row; the 6th row is the repetition of the 2nd row, but it is begun (compare the two rows) about the middle of the 2nd row, so as to change the places of the thick diamonds in the following pattern. This will be easily understood in the course of the work.

258. Pattern for Knitted Curtains.

Knitted Insertion

Material: Messrs. Walter Evans and Co.'s knitting cotton No. 20 or 30.

Cast on 14 stitches, and knit in rows, backwards and forwards, as follows: 1st row: Slip 1, knit 2 together, throw cotton forward, knit 2, knit 2 together, throw cotton forward, knit 2, knit 2 together, throw cotton forward, knit 3. This row is repeated 18 times more; the stitch formed by throwing the cotton forward is knitted as 1 stitch.

20th row: Slip 1, knit 2 together, make 1, knit 1; place next 3 stitches upon another needle behind the cotton, and leave them alone; knit 1, knit 2 together, throw cotton forward, now knit the first 2 of the 3 stitches which have been left; knit the last of the 3 together with the next stitch on the needle, throw cotton forward, knit 3. Repeat these 20 rows till strip is long enough.

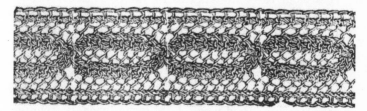

259. Knitted Insertion.

Knitted Cover for Sofa Cushion

Materials: Messrs. Walter Evans and Co.'s knitting cotton No. 12; eight ply fleecy wool.

This cushion (15 inches wide, 12 inches high) is made of grey calico; it is covered on one side with knitting, worked with grey crochet cotton. The knitted cover has an open-work pattern, worked backwards and forwards on a number of stitches which can be divided by 2, and which must suit the width of the cushion, in the following manner: 1st row: Alternately throw the cotton forward, knit 2 together.

260. Stitch for Sofa Cover.

2nd row: Slip 1, knit the other stitches. The stitch formed by throwing the cotton forward is knitted as 1 stitch.

261. Sofa Cushion.

3rd row: Knit 1, * throw the cotton forward, knit 2 together. Repeat from *; after the last decreasing knit 1.

4th row: Like the 2nd row.

These four rows are repeated till the cover is sufficiently large. Draw a narrow piece of red worsted braid through every other open-work row of the pattern, as can be seen in illustration 260. When the cushion has been covered with the knitting, it is edged all round with a border knitted the long way, in the above-mentioned open-work pattern; it is 14 rows wide, and also trimmed with worsted braid: a fringe of grey cotton and red wool, 3 1/4 inches wide, is sewn on underneath the border at the bottom of the cushion; to this is added a thick red worsted cord, by which the cushion is hung on over the back of an arm-chair. The cushion, on account of its simplicity, is especially suitable for garden chairs.

Knitted Pattern

Materials: Messrs. Walter Evans and Co.'s knitting cotton No. 20 for couvrettes, or Berlin wool for sofa quilts.

This pattern can be worked either in wool or cotton, and is suitable for many purposes. Cast on a sufficient number of stitches, divided by 18, for the 1st row: Knit 4, throw the cotton forward, knit 2 together, throw the cotton forward knit 2 together, knit 4, purl 6, repeat from *.

2nd row: The stitches knitted in the 1st row are purled as well as the stitches formed by throwing the cotton forward; the purled stitches are knitted. This row is repeated alternately, therefore we shall not mention it again.

3rd row: * Knit 6, throw the cotton forward, knit 2 together, throw the cotton forward, knit 2 together, knit 6, purl 2.

5th row: Purl 4, * knit 4, throw the cotton forward, knit 2 together, throw the cotton forward, knit 2 together, knit 4, purl 6.

7th row: Knit 2, * purl 2, knit 6, throw the cotton forward, knit 2 together, throw the cotton forward, knit 2 together, knit 6.

9th row: Knit 2, * purl 6, knit 4, throw the cotton forward, knit 2 together, throw the cotton forward, knit 2 together, knit 4.

11th row: * Knit 6, purl 2, knit 6, throw the cotton forward, knit 2 together, throw the cotton forward, knit 2 together.

13th row: Throw the cotton forward, knit 2 together, * knit 4, purl 6, knit 4, throw the cotton forward, knit 2 together, throw the cotton forward, knit 2 together.

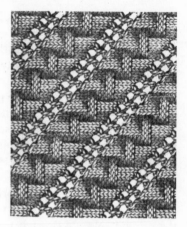

262. Knitted Pattern.

15th row: * Throw the cotton forward, knit 2 together, throw the cotton forward, knit 2 together, knit 6, purl 2, knit 6. The knitting can now be easily continued from the illustration.

Knitted Shawl

Materials: Shetland wool, white and scarlet; steel needles.

This shawl is knitted in the patterns given on Nos. 346 and 347. Both illustrations show the patterns worked in coarse wool, so as to be clearer. Begin the shawl, which is square, on one side, cast on a sufficient number of stitches (on our pattern 290); the needles must not be too fine, as the work should be loose and elastic.

Knit first 2 rows plain, then 3 of the open-work row of pattern No. 263, which is worked in the following manner: 1st row: Slip the first stitch, * knit 2 together, inserting the needle into the back part of the stitch, slip 1, knit 2 together, throw the wool twice forward; repeat from *.

2nd row: Knit 1 and purl 1 in the stitch formed by throwing

the wool forward in the preceding row; the other stitches are purled. In the next row the holes are alternated – that is, after the 1st slipped stitch knit 1, throw the wool forward, and then knit twice 2 together. When 3 such open-work rows are completed, knit 1 row plain, and then work the pattern seen on No. 264, which forms the ground, and is worked in the following way: 1st row: Slip the 1st stitch, alternately throw the wool forward, and decrease by slipping 1 stitch, knitting the next, and drawing the slip stitch over the knitted one.

2nd row, entirely purled.

When 6 such rows have been worked in this pattern, work again 9 rows of the open-work pattern, but work on each side of the 2 stripes, each 6 stitches wide, in the pattern of the ground (No. 264); each first stripe is at a distance of 4 stitches from the edge, and each second stripe at a distance of 20 stitches. After the 9th open-work row, work again 6 rows

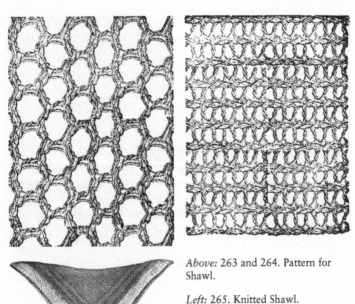

Above: 263 and 264. Pattern for Shawl.

Left: 265. Knitted Shawl.

in the pattern of the ground, then again 8 open-work rows, and then begin the ground, only continue to work on both sides of the shawl the narrow stripes of the ground pattern, the narrow outer and the two wide inner stripes of the border in the open-work pattern. When the ground (pattern No. 264) is square, finish the shawl at the top with two wide and one narrow open-work row, as at the bottom, divided by stripes in the ground pattern. Knot in, all round the shawl, a fringe of scarlet wool; the fringe must be 3-½ inches deep.

About the Author

Isabella Beeton was born Isabella Mary Mayson on 12 March 1836 in Cheapside, London. Her father died when she was young, after which her mother remarried. The family moved to Epsom, Surrey, where Isabella grew up. She attended a school in Heidelberg, Germany, for two years before returning to Epsom, where she taught piano and worked in a local confectioners making pastries. It was living in a huge family – she was the eldest of twenty siblings – that gave her the experience in household management that informed her writing.

Isabella married Samuel Beeton, a wealthy publisher of books and magazines, in 1856. After their continental honeymoon they moved into his large villa in Hatch End, Pinner. She began to write articles on household management for her husband's publishing company a few months after their marriage, notably writing a monthly supplement to *The Englishwoman's Domestic Magazine* in 1859–61. It was these articles that formed the first volume of her most famous book, *The Book of Household Management*, which contained recipes and advice on everything from childcare and recruitment of servants to entertainment and etiquette. It was very much the forerunner of our modern recipe books, with illustrations on almost every page and a clear and informative layout.

In 1861 Isabella's husband set up a new weekly ladies' magazine called *The Queen*, which initially detailed fashionable London social events and high society. Isabella visited Paris to establish a French market for the magazine, and, possibly as a consequence of this, it evolved into a fashion-conscious magazine showing readers the latest French fashions and providing patterns that could recreate them. Isabella was an accomplished needlewoman and published *Beeton's Book of Needlework*, showing the middle class housewife how to tat lace, embroider, crochet and knit. Much of her writing catered to the rising middle classes, who aspired to the quality of living of the upper classes but who had to manage their own households.

After giving birth to four children, Isabella contracted puerperal fever and died in 1865, aged only twenty-eight. Her husband's publications increasingly became involved in controversy and he was forced to sell off his business. He died twelve years after his wife in 1877 and was buried with her in West Norwood Cemetery.

Although best known as the woman behind the modern recipe book, Isabella had an opinion on all aspects of home maintenance. She drew on her experiences to provide the rising middle classes with clear instructions on everything from how to bring up their children to how to create their own fashionable crochet accessories.